Human Growth and Development

Oxford University Press, Walton Street, Oxford OX2 6DP

OXFORD LONDON GLASGOW NEW YORK
TORONTO MELBOURNE WELLINGTON CAPE TOWN
IBADAN NAIROBI DAR ES SALAAM LUSAKA ADDIS ABABA
KUALA LUMPUR SINGAPORE JAKARTA HONG KONG TOKYO
DELHI BOMBAY CALCUTTA MADRAS KARACHI

British Library Cataloguing in Publication Data
Human growth and development. — (Wolfson College.
   Lectures ; 1976).
   1. Child development
   I. Bruner, Jerome Seymour   II. Garton, Alison
   III. Series
   155.4   BF721   77-30416

   ISBN 0-19-857517-3
   ISBN 0-19-857518-1 Pbk

Typeset by Hope Services, Wantage
Printed in Great Britain
by J. W. Arrowsmith Ltd., Bristol

Human Growth and Development

WOLFSON COLLEGE LECTURES 1976

EDITED BY
JEROME S. BRUNER
AND
ALISON GARTON

CLARENDON PRESS · OXFORD

Contents

Preface

The Wolfson College Lectures bring before the University community topics of general interest that are undergoing growth and transformation as a result of scholarly endeavour. Each of the series of Lectures has sought to examine in depth not only the 'state of the art' in its field but also the implications of new developments for the broader society. In 1976, the College decided upon the topic of human development, and distinguished scholars were invited to present the results of their research and reflection. The lectures are set forth here.

It would be hard to imagine a more timely topic. Reduced population growth in the developed nations, changes in the family, and alterations in our basic values have, in the last half century, stimulated a quickened interest in the cultivation of human capabilities. There has, moreover, been a widespread feeling that the growth of urban, industrial society has threatened not only the quality of life generally, but more specifically the conditions of life necessary for the sound rearing of the young. We note with alarm (or with satisfaction) changes in the new generation. At the same time there have been the demands for higher levels of intellectual skill that grow out of an increasingly complex technology. Are they being met? As perhaps never before in human history, we are troubled about our ways of raising the young.

But, alas, while issues of this order need airing and debate, they also need calm, dispassionate and scholarly enquiry. In this respect we are fortunate. For the study of human development has undergone enormous growth in the last decades, partly no doubt in response to the new concerns of modern society. The enquiries that have emerged from laboratories, clinics and a variety of other research settings have taken many forms. Field and laboratory biologists have explored anew the evolution of immaturity and the way in which the growing years in different species is managed. Investigations of the conditions of primate infancy have been of particular interest to those seeking clues about human development. Professor Hinde's opening lecture explores the primate pattern of social development, and how the young monkey is readied for taking his role in the primate group. Much of the work he reviews is his own or was carried out jointly with students and colleagues in the field or at Madingley, outside Cambridge. The attachment, security and well-being of the primate young depend upon a subtle interplay of social interaction that defies simple generalization.

In the second lecture, Professor Rutter pursues many of the same themes, focusing on the human child. He poses his question in a challenging way: what appear to be the conditions, when all the social indicators combine to make a poor prognosis for healthy development, that seem nonetheless to help the child toward healthy growth? His lecture brings together many strands of research hitherto unexamined concerning the social and communal factors that make possible the realization of human potential—as well as exploring the better known factors that defeat it.

The two following lectures concentrate upon the crucial role played by language acquisition in the intellectual development of the child. Professor Bruner considers the manner in which social interaction between infant and mother leads the child with astonishing speed to 'crack' the complex code of adult language. He examines closely in what sense the acquisition of language can be considered an expression of an 'innate' capacity, and to what extent it is dependent upon a speical and privileged interaction between mother and child. In Dr. Clark's lecture, the emphasis is upon how the child in learning language comes to relate what he says to the context in which he is saying it—the classical linguistic problem of deixis. Whilst she concentrates on how the child manages to learn such simple (though powerful) contrasts as I-you, here-there, this-that and come-go, the lesson that emerges casts in sharp relief the more general issue of how structurally systematic and logically interdependent the categories of language are. The two lectures must leave one with a sense of how intellectually subtle a tool early language is and, in addition, they pose the question of how language can be better used as an instrument of thought and of social interaction.

Professor Inhelder's lecture sets forth new currents in the study of cognitive development at Geneva, one of the world's greatest centres of developmental research, founded by Jean Piaget. She poses the deep question as to when it is that the child, in solving a problem or learning something new, can benefit from experience. It is most often characteristic of the child at any level of development that he benefits only from information that fits the logical and other presuppositions typical of his mental age. How then does he progress beyond? Professor Inhelder's lecture postulates with striking demonstrations some hypotheses about what creates the conditions of 'openness' and 'closedness' to new information during intellectual development in children.

In the final lecture, Professor Tizard looks at the state of care of the young in modern society. He takes his departure from the puzzling question of the balance that exists in modern society between the family and other institutions in caring for young children. Given that women increasingly seek and find employment and that the number of women in employment during the infancy and early childhood of their children steadily increases, how should society provide care for these children? And how, indeed, does the society provide some relief for some time each day for the mother not at work but locked in the isolation of an urban and anonymous community? Questions of this order, moreover, take on a degree of immediacy when looked at in the light of what we are beginning to learn about the development of emotional security, language and intellectual competence in childhood.

Unfortunately, one of the lectures delivered in the series is not included in this volume. Professor Basil Bernstein wished further to develop the ideas he presented and to delay publication. The Editors wish to thank the lecturers who participated for their generous co-operation. We must also thank our colleagues on the College Lecture Committee, Dennis Gath, Donald Broadbent and Michael Argyle for their help, the President and Lady Fisher for their lively participation in all the arrangements and Mr. Boddington who assured each week that the College was fit for eye and ear at the time of the lectures. And last but by no means least, we thank Mrs. Meg Penning-Rowsell who edited the manuscripts for publication with such care.

Wolfson College   Jerome Bruner
Oxford   Alison Garton

1 Social Development: A Biological Approach*

ROBERT A. HINDE

INTRODUCTION

I presume I was asked to speak first in this series of lectures on 'Human Growth and Development' because much of my work has been with non-human primates, and there is a feeling around that monkeys 'came first'. I decided that it would not be useful for me to attempt to present a picture of social development in non-human primates—the generalizations would be accompanied by too many exceptions. Nor would it be valuable to list the innumerable, and often trivial, parallels between social development in monkeys and man, nor to emphasize the ways in which man differs from all other species. Instead I shall pick out a number of issues arising from studies of non-human primates that seem to be important for, and in some cases somewhat neglected in, studies of human social development.

That studies of monkeys should be relevant in any way to studies of human social development might well be doubted on a number of grounds. Biologists, who are trained to be conscious of the diversity of nature, know that projections from one species to another can be misleading. And that issue is compounded here by the diversity of the circumstances surrounding infancy both amongst non-human primates and amongst human cultures. There can be no simple comparison of man and monkey. Of course one could embark on a search for universals, but universals in the sense of facts that are

*This work was supported by the Royal Society, the Medical Research Council, and the Grant Foundation. I am grateful to P. P. G. Bateson, J. Dunn, and N. W. Humphrey for their comments on the manuscript, and to C. Berman, J. Ingram, and R. Seyfarth for allowing me to use unpublished material.

true for all primates can be rather trivial. Of more interest would be the dimensions of variation, and how they are related to each other. As yet, however, we know too little about too few non-human primates to get very far with such an approach (but see Blurton Jones, 1976). Another difficulty concerns the prepotent importance of language in all human cultures. This is crucial even for studies of infancy and childhood, for a number of reasons. There is increasing evidence that human infants are predisposed in a number of ways to acquire verbal language—in the sounds and in the auditory discriminations (e.g. Eimas *et al.*, 1971; Eisenberg, 1969) that they make, and in many aspects of their early non-verbal communication (e.g. Stern, 1974), as well as in their potential for cognitive development. Many aspects of human mother–infant interaction facilitate the acquisition of language (e.g. Bruner and Sylva, in press): these include many details of their non-verbal, preverbal, and verbal interactions, the complexity and subtlety of the ways in which each responds to the other, and the tendency of parents to behave towards their infants in accordance with a framework of meaning presumed to be shared between them (e.g. Newson, 1974; Stern, 1974, Trevarthen, 1974). For such reasons, many aspects of the social development of human infants cannot be understood unless their probable consequences for language development are recognized. Furthermore, language has made possible the cultural differentiation which man displays. The aims of human parents are influenced by the pressures and sanctions to which they are exposed in their culture. They can aim to 'be good parents' or 'to create a good parent–child relationship' to an extent inconceivable in a chimpanzee.

Having thus I hope made clear the limitations of my position, I intend to spend the rest of my time showing that it is not altogether untenable. There are some universals which, if one hits the right level of analysis, are worth pursuing. More often comparisons of processes are revealing—that is, comparisons of the relations between independent and dependent variables, and how those relations are affected by other variables; processes are more likely to be similar between species than are, say, the relative effectiveness of particular independent variables. And over some issues it is possible to exploit the fact that non-human primates lack some of man's most important attributes to throw light on the human case.

This attempt to exemplify some of the ways in which studies of development in non-human primates are relevant to the human case is based on my own research interests, and does not attempt to cover the literature. Over many issues, I shall leave it to the reader to draw such human parallels as he thinks fit. But where parallels seem appropriate, one must of course beware of assuming that similarities in behaviour imply similarities in mechanism, and one must certainly not assume that, where there is variability within or between human cultures, practices closer to the non-human primate condition are to be preferred.

1. CONTACT COMFORT

All monkeys and apes—and I am excluding from this discussion the more primitive prosimians—spend the greater part of their early life in physical contact with another individual. Young infants usually cling to their mothers in a ventro-ventral position, which gives them ready access to the nipple when the mother is seated, and enables them to use the nipple as a fifth point of support when the mother is walking or climbing. Later they often ride dorsally or cling to their mother's neck. That frequent physical contact with the mother lasts for a considerable part of their developmental years is illustrated for one species in Fig. 1: the data were obtained in a study of free-living rhesus monkeys on Cayo Santiago by Ms. C. Berman, and I am grateful to her for allowing me to use them here. Furthermore, it has been established experimentally that contact with the mother or mother surrogate can be comforting in anxiety-provoking situations (Harlow and Zimmerman, 1959).

I have raised this now rather hackneyed issue of 'contact comfort' to illustrate the caveat at the end of the previous section. The ubiquity of physical contact between mother and infant in other primate species does not of course mean that human babies must have near-continuous physical contact with an adult. In many cultures they do, but equally in

Relate it to school → show the child affection → he'll like it.

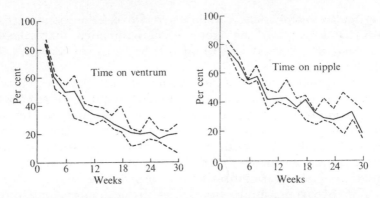

Fig. 1. Mother–infant interaction in rhesus monkeys. Median and inter-quartile range of time on ventrum and time on nipple. Data obtained at Cayo Santiago and reproduced by permission of Carol Berman.

many cultures they do not. In each society a whole complex of practices has, through the joint action of biological and cultural forces, become more or less standardized to meet the baby's needs. In comparing cultures or species one must compare those complexes of practices in the contexts in which they occur, and not independent aspects of child care. But the ubiquity of bodily contact between infant and care-giver in primates does give a certain perspective to some facts about babies—for instance that swaddling and rocking can soothe, how readily children become attached to blankets or soft toys with which they have contact in bed, and the efficacy of the dummy. Furthermore, observations in a culture where babies are carried in bodily contact with their mothers indicate that many infant reflexes function to re-adjust position on the mother, or to grasp the mother as she gets up or moves off (Konner, 1972; Blurton Jones, 1974). Perhaps even such trite 'universals' derived from studies of non-human primates are not without value if they integrate a number of facets of infant development.

2. SOCIAL COMPANIONS OTHER THAN THE MOTHER

This physical contact is usually, but not invariably, provided primarily by the mother. In many species, such as the rhesus monkey, the mother does not permit contact between the infant and any other individual for days or weeks after birth. But there are also many species in which infants are regularly handled by other members of the troop. An extreme case is the Hanuman langur, where the mother allows other females to handle the infant within a few hours of birth, and where it may be carried by eight or ten different females in its first two days of life (Jay, 1965). All intermediates between these extremes are to be found. Generalizations are thus difficult, but it is usually true that, amongst females, those most interested in young infants are subadults and adults without young of their own.

The extent and nature of the relationship between infants and individuals other than their mothers varies with the age of the infant, for three reasons. First, in most species infants are most attractive a short while after birth, and indeed they usually possess special physical characteristics at that time which are lost as they grow up. The rhesus monkey has a parting in its head hair, and in other species newborns have a distinctive coat colour. A number of years ago Lorenz (1950) suggested that the same is true of man, and that the attractiveness to man of many animals (especially cartoon animals) depends on their having stimulus characteristics, such as a bulging forehead, in common with human infants: there is some experimental support for this view (Gardner and Wallach, 1965).

There are two other reasons why the amount of interaction between infants and adult females other than their mothers changes as the infant develops. One is that the infant's ability to resist or solicit the attentions of others increases with its age; the other is that mothers tend to become increasingly permissive as the infants grow older. As a result of these factors, in species in which the mothers are restrictive or only moderately permissive other females can at first only inspect infants visually, but later come progressively to touch, groom, cuddle and play with them, and later still to behave aggressively to them (Spencer-Booth, 1968).

The extent to which males interact with infants also varies widely. At one extreme are species like the patas monkey, where the male normally stays somewhat apart from the females in his group and rarely shows any interest in infants (Hall, 1965). At the other lie the gibbons, marmosets, and tamarins, which live in nuclear families where the infant is carried for much of the time by the male. Some illustrative data obtained from captive marmosets are shown in Fig. 2

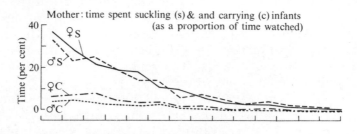

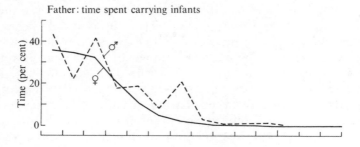

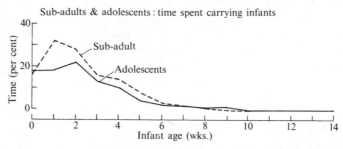

Fig. 2. Proportion of observation time that infant marmosets spend on various social companions. Data for mother show suckling times and carrying but not suckling times separately. Data for mother and father show male and female infants separately. Animals lived in family groups, and were observed during the morning hours. (Jennifer Ingram, 1975.)

(Ingram, 1975). Most species lie between these extremes: the males protect the infants from predators and intruders, show some interest in and considerable tolerance of them, and sometimes interfere in disputes protectively on their behalf, but rarely show anything approaching maternal behaviour (see Mitchell, 1969). However in recent years particularly close relationships between adult males and infants or adolescents have been described in a number of species (e.g. Bertrand, 1969), and in some species males often play with and carry infants. In some of these species (e.g. Barbary macaque, *Macaca sylvana*, Deag and Crook, 1971; Deag, 1974) middle-ranking males seem to carry infants as a 'passport' for approaching another animal in a situation where tension is potentially present. In baboons, male–infant relationships may arise from a previous relationship between the male and the infant's mother, or they may arise de novo (Ransom and Ransom, 1971). Relationships between subadult male hamadryas baboons and female infants develop into consort relationships (Kummer, 1967, 1968).

As the infant develops, interactions with peers become increasingly important and involve primarily the heterogeneous activities known as 'play'. In those species in which mothers and infants spend much time alone, most of the infant's play is non-social or involves the mother: chimpanzees, which live thus for much of the time, also come together into larger groups and peer–peer play is then frequent (e.g. van Lawick-Goodall, 1968). In species which live in groups containing a number of adult females, the young spend much of their time playing with each other: in some such species infants tend especially to play with other infants of similar age and sex (Owens, 1975).

Thus, while the infant's world is formed initially solely by its mother's body, its social world soon extends to a number of other individuals. Its interactions with these other individuals must certainly play a considerable part in its social development. The roles of other females and of the male have, however, been rather neglected in experimental studies, partly because a high proportion of such studies have used the rhesus macaque, in which such individuals normally interact little with infants (Lehrman, 1974). However a considerable amount of experimental work has been directed towards assessing the relative importance of interactions with its mother and with peers in the development of a rhesus monkey. This work has been reviewed in some detail elsewhere, and will not be discussed here (Sackett, 1968; Harlow and Suomi, 1971). It seems to show that the presence of peers is as important or more important for normal development than the presence of the mother—provided, of course, that certain of her essential functions are fulfilled artificially. A reservation concerning this conclusion will be mentioned later.

In the human case, also, attention has centred on the mother-infant relationship and there has been an almost equal neglect of the role of fathers, though interest is now growing (e.g. Lamb, 1976; V. Binney, pers. comm.). The importance of peer-peer relationships is also now increasingly recognized (Lewis and Rosenblum, eds., 1975).

Recognition that the young child may become involved simultaneously in a number of relationships raises a number of further issues. Each type of social companion interacts with the infant in diverse ways. A mother monkey, for instance, provides food, warmth, and contact comfort, support and protection, she grooms and is groomed by the infant, plays with it, and may elicit sexual, aggressive, and fleeing behaviour and so on through a list which could include virtually all the types of social interaction in which monkeys indulge. Each other type of social companion also interacts with the infant in the majority of these ways, though the relative extent of each type of interaction varies with their age/sex category. We usually classify the social influences in terms of the individual who exerts them, and some authors have reified the social relationships of monkeys into infant-mother, maternal, peer, heterosexual and paternal 'affectional systems' (Harlow and Harlow, 1965), though precisely what is meant by a 'system' in this context has not been made clear.

The important problem which arises here can be characterized in terms of two extreme possibilities. It could be that, to the infant monkey, the total amount of each type of interaction in which it engages has an importance that is independent of the type or identity of the individuals with which it interacts: for instance, an infant could be little affected by the absence of peers if its mother played with it enough. At the other extreme, it could be crucial for the infant's social development that it should form relationships of particular types with particular individuals. Bowlby (1969) has argued that the human infant needs to attach himself especially to one caregiver, and it is indeed likely that a continuing peer–peer relationship with one individual will have consequences different in a number of ways from those of interactions with diverse peers—no value judgement being intended.

In one study concerned with this issue four infant rhesus monkeys raised by their own mothers were compared with four infants who were rotated among mothers on a bi-weekly schedule. Although the mothers in the rotated group showed apparently normal social behaviour, the infants showed more 'disturbance' behaviour. They did not, however, show abnormalities in play, social or sexual behaviour (Harlow and Harlow, 1969), and later tended to be higher in social dominance than normally-reared animals (Sackett, 1968). The study is thus inconclusive.

This issue of the importance of 'monotropy' is crucial for the design of child-care facilities. It can be taken as certain that the truth lies with neither of the alternatives posed in the previous paragraph, and there are likely to be consequences, which most would agree to be advantageous, both with having a monotropic relationship with a caregiver and with having diverse social experience. The evidence for the importance of a continuing mother–infant relationship is now considerable (Bowlby, 1969, 1973; Rutter, 1972; Douglas, 1975). But there is also evidence that, under certain circumstances, children brought up in residential nurseries for two years may, if then put into a family environment, show no retardation in intellectual development and come to differ remarkably little in social behaviour from children in nuclear families from the start (Tizard and Rees, 1974, 1975): however the extent of the effects on social behaviour are not yet clear.

3. THE SOCIAL NEXUS

So far the infant's social world has been represented as involving a series of independent relationships. But the various individuals who interact with the infant also interact with each other, and their several relationships may affect each other. The infant is thus born into a pre-existing nexus of social relationships, changes in any one of which may affect many others. For example, how restrictive a mother rhesus monkey is with her infant is affected by the presence of social companions: a subordinate mother can protect her infant from the attentions of others by keeping it near her (Rowell, Hinde and Spencer-Booth, 1964). The extent to which her companions affect her relationship with her infant may depend on her relationship with them—the effect may be small or absent if she is dominant, and a mother may permit her own sister to handle the infant, but not an un-related female. Her relationship with other females may also be affected by their (and her) relationship with the adult male, who might intervene in any dispute on one side or the other (Fig. 3). Tracing the manner in which relationships affect relationships in this way is a task of great complexity, and one with which primatologists are only just beginning to grapple (Hinde, 1972; Hinde and Stevenson-Hinde, 1976; Deag, 1974).

It is because the infant lives in such a complex social nexus that some experiments aimed at assessing the relative importance of the various social companions, and involving raising infants in controlled situations, must be interpreted with caution. Harlow's conclusion about the importance of peer–peer relationships (see above) was based primarily on comparisons between rhesus monkeys brought up alone with their mothers and monkeys brought up without mothers but with one or two peers. While this sounds like a good experimental design, the fact is that rhesus monkeys usually grow up with mothers *and* peers, and indeed with animals of other age/sex classes as well, each affecting the behaviour of all others. Thus the behaviour of a mother living alone with her infant is not the same as that of a mother in a social group. In particular, mothers living alone reject their infants more often than mothers living in social groups (Hinde and

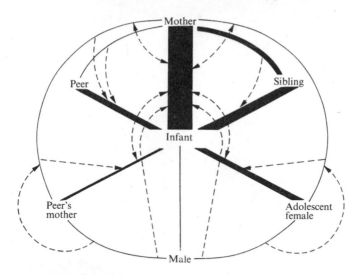

Fig. 3. Diagrammatic representation of the first order zone of an infant monkey. The continuous lines represent relationships, their thickness roughly indicating their importance to the infant. The discontinuous lines represent those effects of relationships on relationships for which quantitative or reasonably firm qualitative data have been obtained.

Spencer-Booth, 1967). Thus comparisons between the two restricted social situations may not indicate the consequences of interactions with the several social companions in the natural troop.

The arrival of an infant may itself have a dramatic effect on the nature of the social nexus. Infants, as we have seen, are attractive to other individuals in the troop, and enhance the mothers' attractiveness: at the same time, however, new mothers of many (but not all) species tend to avoid close contact with social companions to a greater extent than they had done previously. As a result of these two tendencies, the mother may spend more or less time with the various other individuals in the group (Hinde and Proctor, 1977), and there may be a marked redistribution of social relationships. Furthermore the changes in social structure resulting from the birth of a baby may depend on other factors. I am grateful to Dr. R. M. Seyfarth (1976) for allowing me to illustrate this with some of his data from a troop of

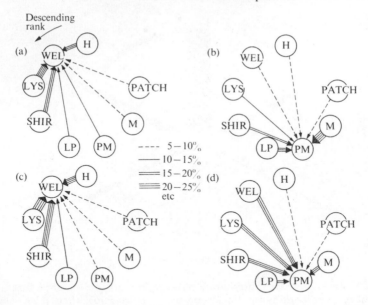

Fig. 4. Grooming amongst the adult females in a troop of baboons. The females are arranged in dominance order anticlockwise, H ranking highest. The lines show the percentage of grooming received by WEL ((a) and (c)) and PM ((b) and (d)) provided by each other female: (a) and (b) represent data obtained before WEL and PM respectively gave birth, and (c) and (d) represent data after that birth. (From Seyfarth, 1976.)

baboons in South Africa. Figure 4 shows the grooming received by two females, WEL and PM, before (upper two figures) and after (lower two figures) their infants were born. The figure shows only females, who are arranged anti-clockwise in order of the dominance hierarchy. WEL, who was high-ranking and thus attractive to other animals, received most of her grooming from other high-ranking females before her infant was born; after birth there was little change. By contrast, PM, who was low-ranking and thus less attractive to others, received very little grooming from high-ranking females before her baby was born but much more afterwards. Thus changes in grooming relations differed according to the rank of the female giving birth.

In man, the difficulties of studying even one dyadic

relationship are daunting enough: to gain an understanding of how relationships affect relationships might seem impossible. Yet it is a matter of common experience that they do, and we may get a very blinkered view of the dynamics of a relationship by studying it in isolation. Whilst I am not competent to review the literature in this field, it is clear that it offers challenging opportunities. Studies as varied as those of Patterson and Cobb (1971), Patterson (1974), and Straus (1974) on violence within families, and of Dunn (in press) on the effects on a firstborn of the arrival of a second-born, indicate the importance of considering dyadic relationships against a background of the social nexus in which they are embedded.

4. THE MOTHER–INFANT RELATIONSHIP

(a) *The Problem*

Since the infant's relationship with its mother, though not all-important, is more important than any other at least during its early weeks of life, and since this has been studied more than any other of the infant's relationships, I am going to consider some of its aspects in some detail. Many of the issues that arise apply equally to other relationships formed by the infant. That we are only just beginning to grope towards a conceptual framework adequate to deal with the developmental dynamics of the mother–infant relationship can be illustrated by a consideration of some views current until quite recently.

Until 1968, most students of child development thought that control in the mother–infant relationship rested firmly in the hands of the mother. For pediatricians this was a natural enough view: after all, they could tell a mother what to do, but not a baby. But in 1968 Bell pointed out that the picture is by no means so simple as that, and that in many respects control of the ongoing interactions rests with the infant. The result has been a number of important studies on the 'effects of the infant on his caregiver' (Lewis and Rosenblum, 1974). By contrast, students of animal behaviour, accustomed to analyzing both the stimuli from the parent that release filial behaviour in the infant and the stimuli from the infant that elicit parental behaviour, already regarded the parent–offspring relationship in terms of mutual influences (review by Harper, 1970). Indeed students of animal behaviour tended to take the opposite view from students of child development, assuming that the temporal course of the relationship was determined by the physical development of the young—a view which, as we shall see later, is equally inaccurate. But even though the mutuality of the parent–offspring relationship is now fully realized, many problems remain. In particular, how can one begin to teaze apart the roles of the two partners in the relationship? If each is continuously influencing the other, a stimulus-response analysis, however sophisticated, is likely to prove inadequate. The following sections contain a few points that contribute towards the solution of this problem.

(b) *Measures of individual propensities vs. measures of the relationship*

First, it is important to recognize that practically any measure we take of the behaviour of mothers and infants together is a measure of their interactions, and not a measure of the behavioural propensities of either mother or infant independent of their relationship with each other. For instance, how long a monkey infant spends off its mother depends on the behaviour of both mother and infant, and how often a mother rejects the infant's attempts to gain the nipple depends in part on how often the infant attempts to make contact (Hinde and Herrmann, 1977). Indeed, these measures may differ markedly between the members of a pair of twins (Spencer-Booth, 1968). The same must surely be true of the measures used in many studies of human mother–infant interaction: how often a mother responds to her infant's advances, or how quickly she responds to its cry, will depend on how demanding it has been in the recent and more remote past.

Such considerations inevitably induce a slight reservation about studies of mother–infant interaction conducted in terms of 'mother measures' or 'infant measures', however much one admires the sophistication of such studies in other respects (e.g. Clarke-Stewart, 1973). This issue has recently been recognized by some students of child development (Dunn, 1975).

(c) *The complexity of the age-changes in the mother–infant relationship*

Whilst the age changes in the mother–infant relationship seem to involve primarily the increasing independence of the infant, they are in fact by no means unidimensional and involve diverse changes in many aspects of the relationship. For example, newborn rhesus monkey infants spend all their time on their mothers, but by 25 weeks they are on them for only approximately 30 per cent of the morning hours (Fig. 1). This would seem to imply that the relationship is becoming more distant with age. At the same time, however, it is becoming better 'meshed', in the sense that each partner tends to direct its behaviour according to the ongoing behaviour of the other. For example, the infant becomes less likely to attempt to make ventro-ventral contact with the mother when she is not ready for it, and she becomes less likely to attempt to pick him up when he does not want to come (Hinde and White, 1974). Thus over the same period in which mother and infant are spending less and less time together, their behaviour is also becoming better integrated. The relationship becomes in some ways more distant, and in others more intimate.

That age changes in the relationship are complex in the human case hardly needs saying, but it is necessary to be constantly aware of the dangers of describing them merely in terms of unitary variables, such as increasing 'independence' or 'intimacy'.

(d) *Relative roles of mother and infant in the age changes in the relationship*

The decrease in the time that mother and infant spend together reflects in part the increasing physical capacities of the infant, and might seem to be a direct consequence of its growing abilities and increasing interest in its social and physical environment. However the rate at which the infant attains independence is determined more immediately by changes in the mother than by changes in the infant. In rhesus monkeys, the increase in the time the infant spends off its mother is accompanied in the early weeks by an increase in the frequency with which the mother rejects its attempts to gain contact (Fig. 5). If the increase in indepen-

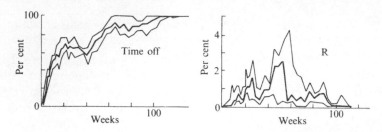

Fig. 5. Mother–infant interaction in rhesus monkeys. Median and inter-quartile range of time off the mother and frequency with which mother rejected infant's attempts to gain contact. Data obtained from small captive groups.

dence were due solely to changes in the infant, the opposite would be the case: it would attempt to gain contact less often and thus be rejected less often. Changes in the mother's behaviour thus play an important part in promoting the independence of her infant (Hinde, 1969, 1974). This view is in harmony with the earlier finding that infants brought up on inanimate surrogate mothers show a slower decrease in the frequency of bodily contacts than do infants reared by their own mothers, presumably because the surrogates do not reject them (Hansen, 1966).

This emphasis on the mother's role in the increasing independence of her infant does not imply that the infant would not achieve independence if the mother took no action: as we have seen, infants reared on inanimate mothers do achieve independence in the end. Nor is it implied that the changes in the mother's behaviour arise endogenously. They may be initiated by changes in the infant's behaviour, such as its increasing demand for milk or its more vigorous locomotor play. But it does seem clear that it is the changes in the mother that immediately regulate the speed with which independence is achieved.

With the proper emphasis on the importance of parental care for human children, there has recently been rather little emphasis on the human parent's role in promoting the child's independence (but see Bowlby, 1969), though this was less true in the earlier literature (Sears *et al.*, 1957). Yet permitting and promoting independence is surely as much part of

the parent's task as nurturing and protecting. On an anec-
dotal level it would seem that mothers do in fact move their
babies from liquid food to solid, from cot to bed, and from
home to school long before the child itself demands or could
demand these changes. And in our society at least an over-
protective mother is almost as much condemned as an over-
rejecting one.

A new perspective on this issue has recently been provided
by the functional considerations advanced by R.L. Trivers.
In brief, the argument is as follows. In evolution, the selective
value of a genetic change will depend not only on the effect
of that change on the individual involved, but also on its
effect on the reproductive success of all related individuals,
appropriately devalued by their relevant degree of related-
ness. Effect is to be measured in terms of both benefit and
cost: in theory it is possible to assess, for any behavioural
interaction, the benefit and cost to each individual in terms
of the effects on their eventual reproductive success. In the
mother–infant relationship, benefit to the mother is to be
measured in terms of the eventual reproductive success of
the current offspring, cost in terms of any reduction, resulting from her investment in the current offspring, in the
probable reproductive success of future offspring. Benefit
to the infant is in his own reproductive success, cost in any
reduction in the reproductive success of his unborn siblings.
As the infant grows, the cost to the mother of nursing increases and the benefit to the infant decreases. If cost and
benefit are measured in the same units, cost to the mother
will come to exceed the benefit to the infant, so that the
mother's long-term reproductive success will decrease if she
continues to nurse. The cost to the mother will affect the
long-term reproductive success of the infant only half as
much as it will affect the mother's, since only half their
genes are shared. Thus until the cost to the mother is more
than twice the benefit to the infant, the infant's overall
fitness will continue to be higher than if he did not suckle.
Thus between the time when benefit and cost to the mother
are equal, and the time when the cost becomes twice the
benefit, natural selection will favour the mother's halting
maternal behaviour and the infant's eliciting it. By an exten-

sion of this argument which cannot be pursued here, Trivers has shown that, on any reasonable assumptions, the infant is selected to demand more parental investment than the parent is selected to provide throughout the period of dependency. Thus the situation that has been found to occur in rhesus monkeys—namely that the mother plays an important part in promoting the independence of the infant—is just that which would be expected on the basis of modern evolutionary theory. Furthermore, some conflict between mother and child is not just an artefact of civilization.

(e) *Towards understanding the dynamics of the changes in the relationship*

We have seen that the mother–infant relationship is a continuing series of interactions between mother and infant, with each contributing to changes in the other as development proceeds. Such a relationship, in which change is continuous, in both partners, which involves diverse features of the morphology and behaviour of both partners, and which varies in rate from time to time, cannot be pictured as a series of successive actions by each partner on the other. How then can we teaze apart the roles of mother and infant in this dynamic relationship? There is no clear answer to this question, but one thing is certain: woolly questions about 'the nature of development' will not help us. Rather must we be hard-headed, specifying the nature of the questions we ask very precisely. This can be illustrated by considering two measures of the mother–infant relationship in rhesus monkeys. The first is a measure of the proportion of the time that an infant is off its mother that it spends outside arm's reach (say 60 cm) of her. The second is a measure of the relative role of the infant in determining the proportion of time that the two animals spend near each other. This is obtained by recording the number of occasions on which one animal approaches the other (i.e. the distance between them decreases from more than 60 cm to less) and the number of occasions on which one leaves the other (i.e. distance increases). The number of approaches due to movement by the infant (Ap_I) as a percentage of the total number of Approaches $(Ap_I + Ap_M)$ (i.e. $100 Ap_I/(Ap_I + Ap_M)$), less the percentage of Leavings due to movement by the infant

$(100 L_I/(L_I + L_M))$, will be an index of the relative role of the infant in maintaining proximity. It will be positive if the infant is primarily responsible for proximity (i.e. if the infant is responsible for a higher percentage of approaches than he is of leavings) and negative if the mother is responsible. This index will be referred to as $\%Ap_I - \%L_I$.

We may now consider three questions concerning the dynamics of the mother–infant relationship:

(i) Who is primarily responsible for proximity at any particular age? As argued above, this is shown by the value of $\%Ap_I - \%L_I$. Figure 6 shows that, under the conditions under which the data were collected, the index is negative in the early weeks and later becomes positive. Thus in the early weeks the mother is primarily responsible for proximity, and later the infant is.

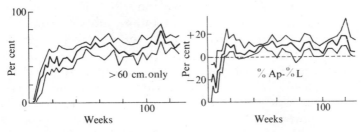

Fig. 6. Mother–infant interaction in rhesus monkeys. Median and inter-quartile range of number of half minutes in which infant was more than 60 cm from mother, and of infant's role in proximity ($\%Ap_I - \%L_I$). Data obtained from small captive groups.

(ii) Are changes in the mother or changes in the infant primarily responsible for the changes, with age, in the time spent in proximity? This can be assessed from the relation between the age changes in the two measures, and the argument is similar to that already given for the time spent in contact. An increase in the time spent at a distance due primarily to a change in the infant would be accompanied by a decrease in the infant's role in proximity. In practice, the increase that occurs with age is accompanied by an increase in the infant's role (i.e. $\%Ap_I - \%L_I$ becomes more positive). The change must thus be due primarily to a change in the mother.

(iii) At any one age, are differences between mother–infant dyads in the extent of proximity due primarily to differences between mothers or to differences between infants? The argument is again rather similar. If they were primarily due to infants, then one would expect that in the dyads in which the infant spent most time at a distance from its mother the infant's role in the maintenance of proximity would be least, and vice versa. In practice the correlations are low, but show consistent age changes: they are positive with young infants, but become negative after about 25 weeks. Thus initially maternal differences are primarily responsible for inter-dyad differences in infant proximity, and later infant differences are responsible (Hinde and Herrmann, 1977).

It will be apparent that the answers to these three questions, which sound deceptively similar, are in fact quite different. It would of course be possible to substitute quite different measures, such as the duration of eye contact between a human mother and her infant, and the same principles would apply. Furthermore, in addition to the types of question discussed so far, it is also possible to ask 'Does this aspect of the relationship at time t affect that aspect at time t + 1?', or 'Does this aspect of partner A's behaviour at time t affect that aspect of partner B's behaviour at time t + 1?'. Such an approach has already been used to good effect in studies of the human mother–infant relationship (Clarke-Stewart, 1973).

Progress in teasing apart the dynamics of the relationship may well depend on asking specific questions of these types, and then asking further questions such as 'In what ways does the mother's behaviour change with age of infant?', or 'In what ways does the behaviour of mothers whose infants spend much time at a distance from them differ from that of mothers whose infants spend little?'. This will lead to further questions, to answer which correlations between measures may again be useful.

Such an approach to the dynamics of relationships is of course basically naturalistic—it involves collecting data about relationships as they develop, and then attempting to account for those data in terms of interactional effects. With non-human species an experimental approach is also possible, and some interesting possibilities are beginning to emerge. For instance, if a rhesus monkey mother is removed from her social group for a few days, leaving the infant in the situation in which it had previously been living, their relationship is greatly disturbed when they are reunited. The infant is at first very demanding, and the mother–infant relationship often goes through a series of stages in which the mother at first accedes, and then becomes rather rejecting, until finally a more-or-less harmonious relationship is established (Hinde, 1969). The data strongly suggest that the behavioural propensities of the participants provide a buffering mechanism on the properties of the relationship such that small divergencies from the course of its development can be corrected, but more gross ones may as it were shift the development of the relationship on to a new course. The evidence so far available has indicated three groups of factors that contribute towards determining whether the separation experience has a long-term effect. First, those infants which before separation were seldom rejected by their mothers, and had to play a relatively small role in staying near them when off them, tend to be less affected. Put colloquially, the less tensionful the pre-separation relationship, the less is that relationship disturbed by the separation experience (Hinde and Spencer-Booth, 1971). Second, infants who remain in the home pen while the mother is removed become depressed more rapidly than infants who are themselves removed whilst the mother stays in the home pen. The reason for this is not certainly understood, but the depression persists after reunion, with the result that such infants are less importunate and less effective in obtaining maternal solicitude. Third, if the mother is removed for the duration of the separation period and the reunion takes place in the home pen, the mother is distracted by her need to re-establish her relationships with other animals in the pen and her maternal solicitude is thereby diminished. Of course additional factors would certainly be revealed by further experiments: all we can say at the moment is that the greatest post-reunion distortion of the mother–infant relationship in our experiments tended to occur when those three factors were combined (Hinde and Spencer-Booth, 1971; Hinde and Davies, 1972). Such data suggest that the mother–infant relationship (and indeed other relationships) has a certain resilience, being capable of self-regulation provided the stresses imposed are not too great, but becoming permanently distorted if they are.

That buffering mechanisms may exist also in human relationships has recently been suggested independently by Dunn (1976). Emphasizing that differences in social or intellectual skills at an early age may be undetectable later, she argues that longitudinal studies are essential if we are to know whether differences at one age really matter subsequently.

One comment on the relationship between the animal and human studies is necessary here. These monkey experiments indicate that infants are more disturbed after reunion if separation had been due to removal of the mother than if the infant itself had been moved elsewhere. Although no comparable human data exist, it seems likely that children would be more upset after reunion if they had been separated from their mother by being sent away from home than if their mother had gone away for a while. If that is the case, the animal and human data would be contradictory. But the contradiction is at the data level: if we abstract a principle from this aspect of the animal data it might be 'Infant distress after reunion is related to how much the mother–infant relationship is disturbed', and this would be true also in man. The disturbance may of course be due to the effects of the separation on the mother or on the infant or on both. That the mother–infant relationship is more distrubed after reunion if the monkey mothers are removed from their infants because they are distracted from their infants by other social factors is an issue more specific to monkeys than to man. Thus the art of extracting the most from comparative studies may lie in finding the right level of abstraction at which to make comparisons. And the only guideline available would seem to be that over some issues comparisons concerned with the processes involved are more likely to be fertile than comparisons of actual data.

(f) *What determines the individual characteristics of a relationship?*

If relationships differ between mother–infant dyads, can we relate the differences to any independent variables—that is, to characteristics of the participants or their situation? Evidence from non-human primates is of three types:

(i) Gross manipulations of the mother can produce gross differences in the mother–infant relationship. For instance infant rhesus monkeys reared on inanimate surrogate mothers have a 'relationship' with them different from the relationships of infants to their real mothers (Hansen, 1966). And if the mother has herself been reared in a bare wire cage, or by a mother who has been reared in a bare wire cage (Mitchell, 1968; Harlow, 1969), the mother–infant relationship may again be quite aberrant.

(ii) Gross manipulations of the social or physical environment can produce measurable differences in the mother–infant relationship. Thus rhesus monkey mothers living alone with their infants tend to be less restrictive than rhesus monkeys living in small caged groups (Hinde and Spencer-Booth, 1967); pigtail macaque mothers punish their infants more in a deprived physical environment than they do if kept in a (relatively) rich one (Jensen *et al.*, 1968); and the difference between animals brought up with and without peers seems to depend on the physical environment (Spencer-Booth, 1969).

(iii) As illustrated also by this last example, the consequences on the mother–infant relationship of more subtle differences in mother, infant or environment are often masked by interactions and are in any case difficult to unravel. We recently attempted to analyse the effects of six independent variables (parity of mother, whether mother born in or introduced into our colony, number of infants previously born in colony, dominance status of mother in her group, presence of peers and sex of infant) on the mother–infant relationship in 63 rhesus mother–infant dyads. All but one of the independent variables appeared to affect the relationship; in several cases the effect depended markedly on the age of the infant, and in several cases there were marked interactions between variables. For example, with mothers of intermediate or subordinate status, mothers having their first infant in the colony tended to be less rejecting and more restrictive than mothers having their second or later infant. With mothers who were dominant in their groups, however, this was not the case (White and Hinde, 1975).

The implication of this is clear enough, and perhaps is already well accepted. The generality of studies comparing groups differing in one independent variable must be accepted with caution: the effect of a given independent variable may be affected by the values of others. In the human case the need for caution in making generalizations is even greater, and every investigator is faced with crucially important decisions in selecting his sample—should he attempt to reduce the variance by selecting according to rigid criteria, and risk his conclusions being of only parochial interest, or should he widen his scope and risk effects being obscured by interactions? The problem is of course compounded by our ignorance of which independent variables are and are not significant. This sounds a little like a cry of despair, but there is perhaps a way out. If attention is focussed on the processes of development, of how experiential factors act, the conclusions are liable to have much greater generality.

(g) *Do the inter-dyad differences matter?*

It is even more important to look in the other direction, asking not what are the sources of inter-dyad differences in the relationship, but what are their consequences for the future behavioural propensities of the infant. Here the evidence is even more sparse. Once again, there is a good deal to show that fairly gross distortions in the mother–infant relationship will produce marked differences in the offspring. It is perhaps hardly surprising that infants brought up without mothers, or with mothers who were extremely punishing, grow up to be different from more normally reared controls (Harlow and Harlow, 1969; Sackett, 1968; McKinney *et al.*, 1971). It is important to know that infants brought up by their mothers in the absence of peers subsequently differ in a number of respects from infants brought up with access to peers, though how much the difference is a direct consequences of the absence of peers and how much due to the fact that in the absence of peers the infants behave in a more demanding way to their mothers, who therefore become more rejecting, is still an open issue (see above and Hinde, 1974).

Considering smaller distortions of the infant's social en-

vironment, it has been shown that if an infant rhesus monkey's mother is removed for one or two periods of 6 days
when it is 6-8 months of age, the effects are detectable in
some circumstances up to two years later (Spencer-Booth
and Hinde, 1971). But whether the ordinary variation in
mother–infant relationships produces effects that can be
detected against the background of the effects of the ubiquitous uncontrolled and perhaps uncontrollable variables
is an issue at present unresolved, though work directed to
that end is in progress.

That early separations between human mothers and children can have long-term effects on development, as postulated
by Bowlby (e.g. 1969; see also Rutter, 1972), now seems
established (Douglas, 1975; but see also Quinton & Rutter,
1976). But such effects can only be detected when data from
large samples are available. When such samples are not available, the search for a close relation between particular early
events and a particular type of subsequent development is
likely often to be abortive for two reasons. First, as already
mentioned, the processes of development may be buffered in
such a way that early aberrations are later compensated for
or disappear (Dunn, 1976). Second, as is implicit in every
section of this paper, development is continuous, and may be
affected by diverse factors throughout its course: the search
for determinants of subsequent personality in the environment of infancy or early childhood can lead too easily to a
neglect of equally important events in later childhood or
adolescence. Once again, the most fruitful results seem likely
to come from a search for processes, for understanding the
dynamics of relationships, rather than merely labelling significant independent variables.

ON DESCRIBING RELATIONSHIPS

If we are to study the differences between the relationships of mother–infant dyads, we must have some means of
describing those differences. So far, relatively little attention
has been paid to the problem of describing relationships, yet
some means of classifying the huge variations we see within
each type of relationship that a child forms is clearly essential for understanding social development. If there is to be a

science of inter-individual relationships, it must surely start from a descriptive base. If such a base is to be useful, it must be clear, objective, and verifiable. Yet some of the most important aspects of inter-individual relationships are, to put it mildly, somewhat intangible. He who would describe relationships must thus walk along a knife edge between the pits of objective triviality and subjective imprecision. Yet the task is important. As a preliminary approach an attempt has been made to specify a number of groups of characteristics that may be useful in studying the dynamics of inter-personal relationships (Hinde, 1976; Hinde and Stevenson-Hinde, 1976). These were:

(a) The content of the interactions within the relationship. A mother–infant relationship normally consists of interactions involving nursing/sucking, protection, mutual games, etc.

(b) The number of different types of interactions in the relationship.

(c) Reciprocity vs. complementarity—that is, do the participants behave similarly (simultaneously or alternately) in the interactions, or in a complementary fashion? While peer–peer relationships may be largely reciprocal, the mother–infant relationship consists mostly of complementary interactions. The nature of the complementarity must, however, be specified along a number of dimensions. Of special interest here are the several forms of power that each exerts over the other, and the manner in which they change with age.

(d) The qualities of the component interactions. To describe an interaction, we must describe what the participants do together and also how they do it. Does the mother bath the baby gently or roughly, change it perfunctorily or with tenderness? Such qualities may be specific to interactions in a particular context, valid for all interactions of a particular type, or valid for all interactions in the relationship.

(e) Relative patterning and frequency of interactions. In addition to specifying the nature and quality of the interactions, we must specify their relations with each other. Thus the future course of a relationship in which the mother always played with her baby when it cried might be quite different from one in which the mother went to play with the baby only when it wasn't crying, even though the amount of crying and playing were the same in both. The context of each type of interaction is crucial for its meaning.

(f) Multidimensional qualities. Many quality labels that we use in everyday life, such as a 'loving relationship', depend on the concurrence of a number of different characteristics. Attempts to specify the latter, and to examine the extent to which they are in fact correlated, may be a useful way of selecting from amongst the almost infinite number of things about a relationship that we could measure.

(g) Cognitive and moral levels. Seen against a background of inter-individual relationships in general, one of the most peculiar things about the mother–child relationship is the marked discrepancy in cognitive and moral levels between the participants. Cognitive and moral levels can now be assessed with at least some degree of objectivity (Kohlberg and Turiel, 1971), and differences in their absolute and relative levels are clearly related to differences in the natures of relationships.

(h) Penetration, or the degree of intimacy in the relationship. This again is a character (or group of characters) which it now is becoming possible to study with some degree of objectivity (Altman and Taylor, 1973). In the mother-infant relationship it clearly changes in degree and in its reciprocity vs. complementarity with age, and differs between dyads.

Of course this list of categories is neither exhaustive nor definitive: its purpose is merely to emphasize that hard-headed descriptions of intangible-seeming relationships are not beyond the bounds of possibility.

6. CONCLUSION

The issues selected for discussion here are all issues that arose from the study of non-human primates. For that reason alone they could be relevant only to certain aspects of human social development. But I hope that they do illustrate some of the ways in which comparative material can help. Of course, to understand man you must study man. But over many issues man's complexity is baffling, and an approach can be mapped out in a simpler species. Indeed in so many aspects of human behaviour, including parent–child relationships, cultural and biological determinants are so closely interwoven that they can be untangled only by comparing man with non-man, in whom cultural influences are at any rate less prepotent. And if comparisons are to be fertile, it would seem to be crucial to focus on the processes of development, on how the dynamic changes in and stability of relationships can be understood, rather than on the roles of particular variables.

REFERENCES

ALTMAN, I. and TAYLOR, D. A., *Social Penetration. The Development of Interpersonal Relationships.* New York and London: Holt, Rinehart and Winston, 1973.

BERTRAND, M., 'The behavioural repertoire of the stumptail macaque.' *Bibliotheca Primatologica,* 11, 1–273, 1969.

BELL, R. Q., 'A reinterpretation of the direction of effects in studies of socialisation.' *Psychological Review,* 75, 81–5, 1968.

BLURTON JONES, N. G., 'Ethology and early socialisation.' In M. P. M. Richards (ed.), *The Integration of a Child into a Social World,* Cambridge University Press, 263–93, 1974.

BLURTON JONES, N. G., 'Growing points in human ethology: another link between ethology and the social sciences?' In P. P. G. Bateson and R. A. Hinde (eds.), *Growing Points in Ethology.* Cambridge University Press, 1976.

BOWLBY, J., *Attachment and Loss. Vol. 1. Attachment.* London: The Hogarth Press, 1969.

BOWLBY, J., *Attachment and Loss. Vol. 2. Separation: Anxiety and Anger.* London: The Hogarth Press, 1973.

BRUNER, J. S. and SYLVA, K. *Acquiring the Uses of Language.* Oxford University Press, in press.

CLARKE-STEWART, K. ALLISON, 'Interactions between mothers and their young children: characteristics and consequences.' *Monographs of the Society for Research in Child Development,* 38, Serial number 153, Nos. 6–7, 1973.

DEAG, J. M., 'A study of the social behaviour and ecology of the wild Barbary macaque, *Macaca sylvana.*' Unpublished Ph.D. thesis, Bristol University, 1974.

DEAG, J. M. and CROOK, J. H., 'Social behaviour and "agonistic buffering" in the wild BArbary macaque, *Macaca sylvana.*' *Folia Primatologica,* 51, 183–200, 1971.

DOUGLAS, J. W. B., 'Early hospital admissions and later disturbances of behaviour and learning.' *Developmental Medicine and Child Neurology,* 17, 456–80, 1975.

DUNN, J., 'Consistency and change in styles of mothering.' *Ciba*

Foundation Symposium—Parent-Infant Interaction, ASP, Amsterdam, 155-76, 1975.

DUNN, J., 'How far do early differences in mother–child relations affect later development.' In P. P. G. Bateson and R. A. Hinde (eds.), *Growing Points in Ethology*, Cambridge University Press, 1976.

DUNN, J. Changes in family relationships with the birth of a sibling. In Proceedings of the IV Biennial Congress of the Int. Soc. for the Study of Behavioural Development. (in press).

EIMAS, P. D., SIQUELAND, E. R., JUSCZYK, P. and VIGIRITO, J., 'Speech perception in infants.' *Science*, 171, 303-6, 1971.

EISENBERG, R. A., 'Auditory behaviour in the human neonate: functional properties of sound and their ontogenetic implications.' *International Audiology*, 8, 34-45, 1969.

GARDNER, B. T. and WALLACH, L., 'Shapes of figures identified as a baby's head.' *Perceptual and Motor Skills*, 20, 135-42, 1965.

HALL, K. R. L., 'Behaviour and ecology of the wild patas monkey, *Erythrocebus patas*, in Uganda.' *Journal of the Zoological Society of London*, 139. 283-327, 1965.

HANSEN, E. W., 'The development of maternal and infant behaviour in rhesus monkeys.' *Behaviour*, 27, 107-49, 1966.

HARLOW, H. F., 'Age-mate or peer affectional systems.' In D. Lehrman, R. Hinde and E. Shaw (eds.), *Advances in the Study of Behaviour, Vol. 2*, New York: Academic Press, 333-83, 1969.

HARLOW, H. F. and HARLOW, M. K., 'The affectional systems.' In A. M. Schrier, H. F. Harlow and F. stollnitz (eds.), *Behaviour of Nonhuman Primates*, Vol. 2. London and New York: Academic Press, 1965.

HARLOW, H. F. and HARLOW, M. K., 'Effects of various mother-infant relationships on rhesus monkey behaviours.' In B. M. Foss (ed.), *Determinants of Infant Behaviour*, Vol. 4. London: Methuen, 1969.

HARLOW, H. F. and SUOMI, S. J., 'Social recovery by isolation-reared monkeys.' *Proceedings of the National Academy of Science*, 68, 1534-8, 1971.

HARLOW, H. F. and ZIMMERMAN, R. R., 'Affectional responses in the infant monkey.' *Science*, 130, 421-32, 1959.

HARPER, L. V., 'Ontogenetic and phylogenetic functions of the parent–offspring relationship in mammals.' In D. Lehrman, R. Hinde and E. Shaw (eds.), *Advances in the Study of Behaviour, Vol. 3*, New York: Academic Press, 75-119, 1970.

HINDE, R. A., 'Analysing the roles of the partners in a behavioural interaction—mother–infant relations in rhesus macaque.' *Annals of the New York Academy of Science*, 159, 651-67, 1969.

HINDE, R. A., 'Social behaviour and its development in subhuman primates.' In *Condon Lectures. Oregon State System of Higher Education*, Eugene, Oregon, 1972.

HINDE, R. A., *Biological Bases of Human Social Behaviour*. New York: McGraw Hill, 1974.

HINDE, R. A., 'On describing relationships.' *Journal of Child Psychology and Psychiatry*, 17, 1–19, 1976.
HINDE, R. A. and DAVIES, L., 'Changes in mother–infant relationships after separation in rhesus monkeys.' *Nature*, 239, 41-2, 1972.
HINDE, R. A. and HERRMANN, J., 'Frequencies, durations, derived measures and their correlations in studying dyadic and traidic relationships.' In H. R. Schaffer (ed.), *Studies in Mother–Infant Interaction: The Loch Lomond Symposum*. Academic Press, 1977.
HINDE, R. A. and PROCTOR, L. P., 'Changes in the relationships of captive rhesus monkeys on giving birth.' *Behaviour* 61, 304–21, 1977.
HINDE, R. A. and SPENCER-BOOTH, Y., 'The effect of social companions on mother–infant relations in rhesus monkeys.' In D. Morris (ed.), *Primate Ethology*, London: Weidenfelt and Nicholson, 1967.
HINDE, R. A. and SPENCER-BOOTH, Y., 'Effects of brief separation from mother on rhesus monkeys.' *Science*, 173, 111-18, 1971.
HINDE, R. A. and STEVENSON-HINDE, J., 'Towards understanding relationships: dynamic stability.' In P. P. G. Bateson and R. A. Hinde (eds.), *Growing Points in Ethology*, Cambridge University Press, 1976.
HINDE, R. A. and WHITE, L., 'The dynamics of a relationship—rhesus monkey ventro–ventral contact.' *Journal of Comparative and Physiological Psychology*, 86, 8-23, 1974.
INGRAM, J. C., 'Parent–infant interactions and the development of young in the common marmoset (*Callithrix jacchus*).' Unpublished Ph.D. thesis, Bristol University, 1975.
JAY, P., 'The common langur in Northern India.' In I. Devore (ed.), *Primate Behaviour*, New York: Holt, Rinehart and Winston, 1965.
JENSEN, G. D., BOBBITT, R. A., and GORDON, B. N., 'Effects of environment on the relationship between mother and infant pigtailed monkeys (*Macaca nemestrina*).' *Journal of Comparative and Physiological Psychology*, 55, 131-6, 1968.
KONNER, M. J., 'Aspects of the developmental ethology of a foraging people.' In N. J. Blurton Jones (ed.), *Ethological studies of Child Behaviour*, London: Cambridge University Press, 1972.
KUMMER, H., 'Tripartite relations in hamadryas baboons.' In S. A. Altman (ed.), *Social Communication among Primates*. Chicago: The University of Chicago Press, 1967.
KUMMER, H., *Social Organisation of the Hamadryas Baboon*, Chicago: The University of Chicago Press, 1968.
KOHLBERG, L. and TURIEL, E., 'Moral development and moral education.' In G. S. Lesser (ed.), *Psychology and Educational Practice*, Glenview, Ill.: Scott Foresman, 1971.
LAMB, M. E., 'Interactions between eight-month olds and their fathers and mothers.' In M. E. Lamb (ed.), *The Role of the Father in Child Development*, New York: Wiley, 1976.
LAWICK-GOODALL, J. van, 'Behaviour of free-living chimpanzees of the Gombe Stream area.' *Animal Behaviour Monograph*, Vol. 1, part 3, 1968.

LEHRMAN, D. S., 'Can Psychiatrists use Ethology?' In N. F. White (ed.), *Ethology and Psychiatry*, University of Toronto Press, 1974.
LEWIS, M. and ROSENBLUM, L. A. (eds.), *The Effect of the Infant on its Caregiver. Vol. 1 in The Origins of Behaviour Series.* New York and London: Wiley, 1974.
LEWIS, M. and ROSENBLUM, L. A. (eds.), *Friendship and Peer Relations.* New York and London: Wiley, 1975.
LORENZ, K., 'Ganzheit und Teil in der tierischen und menschlichen Gemeinschaft.' *Studium Generale,* 9, 455–99, 1950. ('Part and parcel in animal and human societies. A methodological discussion.') In K. Lorenz, *Studies in Animal and Human Behaviour, Vol. 2.* London: Methuen.
McKINNEY, W. T., SUOMI, S. J. and HARLOW, H. F., 'Depression in primates.' *American Journal of Psychiatry,* 127, 1313–20, 1971.
MITCHELL, G. D., 'Persistent behaviour pathology in rhesus monkeys following early social isolation.' *Folia Primatologica,* 8, 132–47, 1968.
MITCHELL, G. D., 'Paternalistic behaviour in primates.' *Psychological Bulletin,* 71, 399–417, 1969.
NEWSON, J., 'Toward a theory of human understanding.' *Bulletin of the British Psychological Society,* 27, 251–7, 1974.
OWENS, N. W., 'Social play behaviour in free-living baboons, *Papio anubis.*' *Animal Behaviour,* 23, 387–408, 1975.
PATTERSON, G. R., 'Stimulus control in natural settings.' In Jan de Wit and Willard W. Hartup (eds.), *Determinants and Origins of Aggressive Behavior,* The Hague and Paris: Mouton, 1974.
PATTERSON, G. R. and COBB, J. A., 'A dyadic analysis of "aggressive" behaviours.' In J. P. Hill (ed.), *Minnesota Symposium on Child Psychology,* 5, 72–129, 1971.
QUINTON, D. and RUTTER, M. Early hospital admissions and later disturbances of behaviour: an attempted replication of Douglas's findings. *Developmental Medicine and Child Neurology,* 18, 447–59, 1976.
RANSOM, T. W. and RANSOM, B. S., 'Adult male–infant relations among baboons, (*Papio anubis*).' *Folia Primatologica,* 16, 179–95, 1971.
ROWELL, T. E., HINDE, R. A. and SPENCER-BOOTH, Y., 'Behaviour of socially living rhesus monkeys in their first six months.' *Proceedings of The Zoological Society of London,* 143, 609–49, 1964.
RUTTER, M., *Maternal Deprivation Reassessed.* Middlesex: Penguin Books, 1972.
SACKETT, G. P., 'The persistence of abnormal behaviour in monkeys following isolation rearing.' In R. Porter (ed.), *The Role of Learning in Psychotherapy,* London: Churchill, 1968.
SEARS, R. R., MACCOBY, E. and LEVIN, H., *Patterns of Child Rearing.* Evanston, Ill.: Row Peterson, 1957.
SEYFARTH, R. M., 'A study of the social relationships among indivi-

duals in a troop of baboons (*Papio ursinus*).' Unpublished Ph.D. thesis, University of Cambridge, 1976.

SPENCER-BOOTH, Y., 'The behaviour of group companions towards rhesus monkey infants.' *Animal Behaviour*, 16, 541-57, 1968.

SPENCER-BOOTH, Y., 'The effects of rearing rhesus monkey infants in isolation with their mothers on their subsequent behaviour in a group situation.' *Mammalia*, 33, 80-6, 1969.

SPENCER-BOOTH, Y. and HINDE, R. A., 'Effects of brief separation from mothers during infancy on behaviour of rhesus monkeys 6-24 months later.' *Journal of Child Psychology and Psychiatry*, 12, 157-72, 1971.

STERN, D. N., 'The goal and structure of mother–infant play.' *Journal of the American Academy of Child Psychiatry*, 13, 402-21, 1974.

STRAUS, M. A., 'A geneal systems approach to the development of a theory of violence between family members.' In Jan de Wit and Willard W. Hartup (eds.), *Determinants and Origins of Aggressive Behavior*, The Hague and Paris: Mouton, 1974.

TIZARD, B. and REES, J., 'A comparison of the effects of adoption, restoration to the natural mother, and continued institutionalisation on the cognitive development of 4 year old children.' *Child Development*, 45, 92-9, 1974.

TIZARD, B. and REES, J., 'The effect of early institutional rearing on the behaviour patterns and affectional relationships of 4 year old children.' *Journal of Child Psychology and Psychiatry*, 16, 61-73, 1975.

TREVARTHEN, C., 'Conversations with a 2-month old.' *New Scientist*, 2nd May 1974.

TRIVERS, R. L., 'Parent–offspring conflict.' *American Zoologist*, 14, 249-64, 1974.

WHITE, L. E. and HINDE, R. A., 'Some factors affecting mother–infant relations in rhesus monkeys.' *Animal Behaviour*, 23, 527-42, 1975.

2 Early Sources of Security and Competence

MICHAEL RUTTER

INTRODUCTION

There have been a wealth of studies which have looked at delinquency, psychiatric conditions, mental retardation and disorders of all kinds in childhood. As a result we know a lot about the origins of *in*security and *in*competence. We have become aware of the damage done by factors such as marital discord, parental rejection, institutional upbringing and the like. However, we know very much less about the conditions which facilitate *normal* development. There has been a distressing lack of curiosity about the early sources of security and competence. Indeed much of what we know about security and competence is merely the other side of the coin of *in*security and *in*competence. Namely, we are aware that most children who do *not* experience discord, rejection and other serious hazards do *not* develop gross disorders of development. Of course it is very important to know that, but it is not terribly interesting in itself. It is hardly a surprise that children who are well looked after by normal well-adjusted parents with whom they have a good relationship should usually develop normally. That is just what everyone would expect.

But it is vital to recognize that this is a probability statement and by no means a certainty. Some children from good stable homes do not do well. They develop psychiatric disorder or become delinquent or show serious educational problems in spite of everything seeming to be in their favour. That's an important issue but it is not one considered in this paper. Then there is the other group of exceptions, the children from terrible homes who despite a variety of unfortunate experiences come through unscathed and appear to have a stable, healthy personality development. Now, there's a challenge. Children who seem to have everything against them and yet still develop security and competence.

This is a much neglected issue, but one which carries with it a tremendous potential for prevention and treatment. It would be good if Society could ensure that every child had a secure, stable, happy upbringing. This is a most worthwhile goal toward which we should all strive, but it would be hopelessly unrealistic to suppose that it could be achieved. The situation now is that usually we can only tinker with children's circumstances; we can make a bad situation a little less bad or we can introduce some ameliorating influences in the hope that they will alter the balance sufficiently for the child to benefit. This is just when we need knowledge on what enables children to develop normally in spite of stresses and disadvantages. It is not a topic on which much is known, but it is one that has interested me greatly both as a clinician trying to help children and their families and as a researcher concerned to understand human development. In this paper, I will draw attention to some of the research findings on this question and will consider some of the issues and principles involved.

1. PERSONAL RELATIONSHIPS

In doing this I intend to focus primarily on *emotional* security and *social* competence (rather than on intellectual development). There is one further restriction, in that I will pay most attention to the development of personal relationships. There are many good reasons for doing that but there is time to mention only one. Disturbed interpersonal relationships are strongly associated with psychiatric disorder in children and in adults. In childhood, both sociometric and clinical studies have shown that youngsters who fail to make friends, who are not liked by others and who are socially rejected or isolated have a much increased risk of psychiatric problems. Thus, in the Isle of Wight general population survey of 10-year-olds, the description '*not* much liked by other children' was one of the best pointers to the presence of psychiatric disturbance (Rutter, Tizard and Whitmore, 1970).

Other studies, too, have shown that youngsters who have serious trouble getting along with other children are those most likely to exhibit general maladjustment.

However, not only are poor peer relationships a good indicator of current problems, they are also a good predictor of later difficulties. Thus the Rochester Study showed that, of all measures in childhood (at age 6–8 years), sociometric status (and in particular rejection by other children) was much the best predictor of psychiatric illness a dozen years later, at a time when the individuals were young adults (Cowen *et al.*, 1973; Zax *et al.*, 1968). Roff showed much the same relation to the prediction of delinquency. Socially isolated children were the ones most likely to steal, rob, and commit other delinquent acts (Roff *et al.*, 1972). Moreover, even with a group of children who all had psychiatric problems, it seems that disturbed peer relationships were associated with a worse long-term outcome (Sundby and Kreyberg, 1969).

In adult life too, mental disorder has been found to be quite strongly associated with disturbed interpersonal relationships and with marital discord (Quinton, Rutter and Rowlands, 1977; Rutter, Quinton and Yule, in preparation). This has been noted in studies of patient groups but also it has been confirmed in general population studies. In short, in all age groups in which it has been studied, difficulties or abnormalities in personal relationships have been linked with psychiatric problems and mental disorder. Accordingly, there are strong grounds for suggesting that a study of the development of personal relationships and of their beginnings in childhood might be informative in a search for the early sources of security and competence.

2. EARLY SOCIAL DEVELOPMENT

Let us then consider what is known about children's early social development. In the first few months after birth, infants tend to respond in much the same way both to familiar adults and to strangers. However, about the age of 7 months, infants usually develop an attachment to a specific person. There is much individual variation in when this happens and the range extends from about 3½ to 15 months

(Schaffer and Emerson, 1964; Ainsworth, 1967). The attachment is shown in many different ways such as by a greeting response to the person concerned, by distress when the person goes away, by a differential following of the person, by the use of the person as a haven of safety and by reduction of fear in a strange environment when the person is present (Ainsworth, 1967; Stayton *et al.*, 1973). These attachments develop even in children reared in institutions (Stevens, 1975), although they may be somewhat delayed in appearance. Moreover, if a toddler is separated from his parents and is looked after by someone else, even for a period of one to two weeks, he tends to develop fresh attachments to the new caretaker (Robertson and Robertson, 1971).

Much has still to be learned about the factors which influence this development but it is clear that neither feeding nor caretaking is an essential feature. Moreover, bonds do not necessarily develop to the person who spends most time with the child. The intensity of interaction probably has more effect than the duration. Attachment tends to be strongest when someone plays with the child and give him a lot of attention, especially if this is associated with responsiveness and sensitivity to the baby's signals (Ainsworth, 1967; Ainsworth *et al.*, 1971; Schaffer and Emerson, 1964; Stayton and Ainsworth, 1973). Probably sensitive responsiveness is the one quality in any interaction which is most likely to foster attachment. However, a baby's tendency to seek attachments is increased by anxiety and fear, and also by illness and fatigue (Bowlby, 1969; Maccoby and Masters, 1970). Attachments are particularly likely to develop to the person who brings comfort at such times.

All studies have shown that most children develop multiple attachments. However, there is continuing controversy on whether these attachments all have the same meaning. Bowlby (1969) has suggested that there is an innate bias for a child to attach himself especially to *one* figure and that this main attachment differs in kind from those to other subsidiary figures. However, this statement involves two rather different propositions, one of which is supported by the evidence and one of which is not. The first proposition is that the several attachments are not of equal strength and are not freely interchangeable. This is well supported by the findings from several studies which show that there is a persisting hierarchy among attachments, with some continuing to be stronger than others (Schaffer and Emerson, 1964; Ainsworth, 1967). Even in institutions, children tend to have their 'favourite' adult to whom they will go in preference to others (Stevens, 1975). The second proposition is that the first or main attachment differs in kind from all other subsidiary ones. Most research findings suggest that this is *not* the case. The proposition may be tested in two different ways. First, it may be determined whether the function or effects of all attachments are similar in *quality* even though they differ in *intensity*. The evidence indicates that they are. Thus, young children protest or are distressed if the person to whom they are attached leaves them. This has been shown to be so for fathers as well as for mothers (Spelke *et al.*, 1973). Similarly, attachment is demonstrated by the reduction of anxiety in a strange situation when a familiar person is present. This has been demonstrated for sibs Heinicke and Westheimer, 1965) for peers (Kissel, 1965; Schwartz, 1972) and for adult caretakers in a nursery (Arsenian, 1943) as well as for mothers. However, it does not occur with strangers. In addition, infants follow and seek closeness with fathers as well as with mothers, whereas again they do not do so with strangers (Cohen and Campos, 1974).

Second, the proposition may be tested by determining if the difference in intensity of attachment between the person at the top of the hierarchy and the person second in the hierarchy is greater than that between the second and third persons. Stevens (1975) found that in most cases it was not, although in some children it was. The evidence is not decisive but it may be concluded that multiple attachments tend to have rather similar functions in spite of a persisting hierarchy among attachments which differ markedly in intensity.

In the earlier studies there was an implicit assumption that attachment was a unitary concept. Subsequent work has confirmed that there are positive (but quite low) intercorrelations between most of the behaviours said to indicate attachment (Coates *et al.*, 1972; Maccoby and Feldman, 1972, Masters and Wellman, 1974). However, it has also become evident that not all behaviours function in the same way (Rosenthal, 1973; Stayton and Ainsworth, 1973). Probably at least two distinctions need to be made. First, there is the difference between attachment behaviour and persisting bonds. Infants show a general tendency to seek attachments and if familiar figures are absent they soon seek new attachments to other people (Robertson and Robertson, 1971). However, the concept of bonding implies selective attachment (Cohen, 1974) which persists over time even during a period of no contact with the person with whom bonds exist (although of course the child's ability to maintain bonds during an absence is far less in infancy than it is in later childhood). The importance of this distinction was shown in the Harlow experiments with rhesus monkeys. Infants reared in social isolation clung to inanimate models (so-called 'cloth mothers') and rushed back to them when threatened or frightened, as by a blast of air in their face (Harlow, 1958; Harlow and Zimmerman, 1959). The behaviour clearly indicates attachment. However, follow-up studies have indicated that these early attachments to inanimate objects did *not* lead on to normal social relationships in adult life, as peer or parent attachments usually do (Harlow and Harlow, 1969). The difference between human attachment behaviour and bonding is shown by Tizard and Rees's (1975) findings regarding institutional children. Four-year-old children reared in institutions showed *more* clinging and following behaviour than family-reared hildren but also they were *less* likely to show selective bonding or deep relationships.

The second distinction is between secure and insecure bonding (Stayton and Ainsworth, 1973). One of the characteristics of bonding is that it enables children to feel secure in strange situations. The apparent 'purpose' of bonding is to give the child security of relationships in order to stop clinging and following, and in that sense to become detached. Thus, Stayton and Ainsworth (1973) found that the children of sensitive responsive mothers showed more positive greeting on reunion and more following behaviour (suggesting stronger attachments) than those shown by the children of insensitive unresponsive mothers, but they showed *less* crying on separation which suggested that they had a more 'secure' attachment. Similarly, Spelke and his colleagues (1973) found that infants who were least fearful with strangers (and hence most secure) had had the most interaction with their fathers. It is also relevant that Hinde and Spencer-Booth (1970) showed that infant rhesus monkeys who exhibited most distress after separation were those who had experienced most rejection from their mothers and for whom there was the most tension in the infant–mother relationship.

Further research is necessary to sort out the various dimensions of attachment and bonding. However, it may be that bonding is best differentiated from attachment behaviour by the presence of *selectivity* in relationships which persist over time and place. The strength of bonding may be best determined by the degree of *reduction* of distress in a frightening situation when the bonded person is present. The security of bonding, on the other hand, may perhaps be assessed by the relative *lack* of distress following separation or by the extent of moving away from the bonded person in a strange situation (this measurement would obviously have to control for strength of bonding). If this formulation is correct, the implication is that attachment behaviour should be strongest in toddlers but bonding most secure in older children. Furthermore, it implies that an institutional environment with a very large number of caretakers but an ample range of stimulating experiences should foster attachment behaviour but not bonding.

It appears then that infants show a generalized tendency to seek attachments with other people. This is a necessary precursor to the development of personal relationships, but it is not enough in itself. If social development is to proceed normally, it is necessary for selective bonding to occur and for the child to develop discriminating individualized relationships with particular people. Circumstantial evidence suggests that these early selective bonds provide the basis for later social development. However, if development is to proceed optimally, it seems that the bonds must not only be strong but also they must be secure. The nature and quality of these early relationships is probably crucial.

There is one further issue that needs to be considered in relation to bonding, and that is how far this process is restricted to a critical or sensitive period in the first few years of life. Evidence on this point is not conclusive. Certainly in all ordinary circumstances, the first two years of life are the time when initial bonding occurs. If, for some reason, children do not have the opportunity to develop bonds then, they may find it increasingly difficult thereafter to develop stable, selective attachments for the first time (especially after the age of 3 or 4 years). However, the development of first bonds in later childhood will be influenced both by the extent of disadvantage suffered in the preceding years and also by the quality of the environment in later years. Unfortunately, little is known on the nature and limits of this apparently 'sensitive' period for initial bonding. It should be added that once the child has developed bonds for the first time, he can transfer these to other people when he is older—the ability to form bonds is not lost, only perhaps the ability to form bonds for the first time. The same has been found with non-human primates (Mason and Kenney, 1974).

3. DISTURBANCES IN SOCIAL DEVELOPMENT

Let us now turn to some of the factors which are known to lead to disturbances in social development. There are many, but I want to discuss only two: a brief admission to hospital and the experience of family discord.

(a) *Short-term Admissions to Hospital*

Admission to hospital is an experience which may sometimes lead to long-term disorders in psychological development and much more often to acute emotional disturbance. There is good evidence that many (but not all) young children show an immediate reaction of acute distress and crying following admission to hospital (Vernon *et al.*, 1965; Yarrow, 1964) (the period of 'protest'), followed by misery and apathy (the phase of 'despair'), and finally there may be a stage when the child becomes apparently contented and seems to have lost interest in his parents ('detachment' in Robertson's and Bowlby's terms). When the child returns to his parents, he may ignore them at first or turn away or seem to reject them. For several weeks or even months, he is 'difficult', bad-tempered and clinging. He follows his mother everywhere round the house, holding on to her skirts and appearing very reluctant to leave her even for a moment. At the same time, he often seems angry and demanding and may hit out at his parents. In this situation the mother and father may become cross and fed up with the child's tiresome behaviour, and push him away or reprimand him. This usually results in a further increase in the child's clinging and demanding (see Rutter, 1972 and Bowlby, 1975 for references to research).

The long-term consequences of a brief admission to hospital have been studied by Douglas (1975) using the National Survey findings, and also by Quinton and Rutter (1976) using general population studies in London and the Isle of Wight. Both investigations found *no* association between single admissions to hospital of less than a week and any kind of disorder in later childhood or adolescence. However, both studies found that *multiple* admissions, when the first admission had taken place during the pre-school years, were associated with an appreciably increased risk of both psychiatric disorder and delinquency some years later.

(b) *Family Discord*

The second variable I want to consider is family discord. Numerous studies have shown that family discord and disharmony are strongly associated with the development of anti-social problems in the children (Rutter, 1971 and 1972). It is important to note that this association applies to homes which have not been 'broken' by divorce or separation, so that it is indeed the discord which is relevant rather than the break-up of the family as such. For example, both McCord and McCord (1959), in their follow-up of the Cambridge-Somerville study, and more recently West and Farrington (1973) found that delinquency was much more common when there was marital disharmony or serious parental conflict than when family relationships were smoother. In our own studies of adult patients' families (Rutter, 1971) we showed a strong relationship between marital discord and anti-social behaviour in the children. Over the course of four years (during a prospective longitudinal study), 36 per cent

of the children from discordant marriages showed persisting
behavioural deviance at school compared with only 7 per cent
of those from non-discordant marriages at the start of the
study (Quinton, Rutter and Rowlands, 1977). Similarly,
in our general population studies of 10-year-old children
(Rutter, Yule *et al.*, 1975), those youngsters from families
with severe marital discord had an increased rate of both
behavioural deviance at school and also psychiatric disorder
as assessed from detailed parental interviews. Among Isle
of Wight adolescents with a persistent psychiatric disorder,
30 per cent came from homes where the parents had a poor
marriage relationship, compared with only 6½ per cent of
control children without psychiatric disorder (Rutter,
Graham, Chadwick and Yule, 1976). Furthermore, Power
et al. (1974) found that among boys who had already made a
Court appearance for delinquency, those from intact homes
with severe and persistent family problems were more likely
to become recidivist than those from either intact homes
without serious problems or from broken homes.

We may conclude that there is abundant evidence that an
ongoing disturbance in family relationships is associated with
a much increased risk of conduct disorders and delinquency
in the children. Of course it could be argued that family
discord does not have a true environmental effect, but rather
that the impaired relationships reflect genetically determined
personality attributes. However, there is considerable circumstantial evidence against this suggestion (Rutter, 1971; Rutter,
Quinton, and Yule, in preparation). First, genetic factors play
only a small part in the pathogenesis of delinquency (Shields,
1977). Second, even within a group of parents with personality disorder, there is still an association between marital
discord and anti-social disorder in the children. Third, the
association is strongest when the discord directly involves or
impinges on the children. Fourth, children who experience
severe family discord in early childhood are less likely to
show later psychiatric disorder if they subsequently experience harmonious family relationships. In short, the evidence
indicates that, although genetic factors doubtless play some
part (probably particularly in the case of more severe and
persistent disorders), marital discord also has an adverse en-

vironmental influence leading to anti-social disorder in the children.

4. AMELIORATING INFLUENCES

So much for the adverse influences on children's social development. Let us return to the main theme of the factors which facilitate normal development and which lead to security and competence. The two risk factors discussed, namely admission to hospital and family discord, are both variables known to be associated with a much increased risk of psychiatric disorder. However, it is known that many children develop normally in spite of these experiences. We need to consider why this is so and what it is that enables them to overcome their disadvantages and survive unscathed.

(a) *Admission to Hospital: Short-term Effects*

Let us begin with the question of admission to hospital. It is most convenient to discuss the ameliorating factors separately according to their short-term and long-term sequelae.

With respect to the short-term effects, the modifying influences can be considered under three headings: characteristics of the child, experiences during the admission, and what happens after discharge from hospital.

So far as the first of these is concerned, the most obvious and important factor is the age of the child (see Rutter, 1972). Children are most at risk between about 6 months and four years of age. Very young infants do not suffer in the same way from admission to hospital, and as the child grows older, after 4 years of age he is progressively less at risk. Thus, one of the reasons why some children are not adversely affected by hospital admission is simply that they are not at the age when ill effects occur. Clearly, whenever possible, hospital admission should be avoided during the age period of peak risk. Stacey and her colleagues (1970) also found that children who had had brief normal separation experiences (such as staying overnight with friends or relatives, having babysitters, attending nursery school or being left all day with a familiar person) were less likely than other children to be disturbed by hospital admission. Children need to learn to be physically detached from their families even though emotional bonds remain. Stacey's finding needs to be replicated, but it seems that this process is aided by the experience of *graded* separations in happy circumstances. Parents need to introduce their children *gradually* to happy situations in which the child remains with a familiar adult during the time the parent is away. The length of the separation needs to be gauged by the maturity of the child, the security of his relationships, and the familiarity of the setting during the separation. However, given proper attention to these, the evidence suggests that graded happy separations can make it easier for children to cope with less happy separation experiences, such as those presented by hospital admission. In part, it is likely to be a question of the situation being a less strange one because the child is already used to a variety of environments other than his family home. In part, too, it may be that the child will be less distressed by the separation because he has already learned from previous separations that his parents always come back. In this way, his uncertainty and his feeling of loss are likely to be less than those of the child who is separated for the first time.

There is also some evidence which suggests that the effects of hospital admission or other forms of stressful separation are worse for children with *insecure* bonds or with poor family relationships. The importance of prior parent–infant relationships in terms of the infant's response to separation experiences is shown most strongly by animal studies. Hinde and Spencer-Booth (1970) clearly demonstrated that infant rhesus monkeys showed much more disturbance following separation if there had been maternal rejection and a tense mother–infant relationship before the separation. A detailed analysis of the findings indicated that much of the post-separation distress was a direct consequence of interference with harmonious parent–infant relationships. Human evidence is meagre but both short-term (Fagin, 1966; Vernon *et al.*, 1965) and long-term (Quinton and Rutter, 1976) studies suggest that emotional disturbance following hospital admission is more likely if the child has a poor relationship with his parents or comes from an unhappy, unstable home. The child's ability to cope well with acute stresses is much influenced by the quality of his long-term family relationships and by the security of his emotional bonds. Insecure children from unhappy homes are probably especially likely to suffer from stressful separations and, conversely, secure children from happy homes are those who are most likely to survive the experience without damage.

A variety of factors during hospital admission also influence the way children respond. First, there is the maintenance of contact with their parents. The observation that distress does not occur below the age when attachments first develop and that distress becomes less frequent at the age when attachment behaviour is waning suggests that the distress may be the result in part of an interference with attachment. This suggestion is supported by the evidence that the distress associated with hospital admission is much less if the children are admitted with a parent (Fagin, 1966; Vernon *et al.*, 1967). Distress may also be reduced by daily visiting (Faust *et al.*, 1952; Illingworth and Holt, 1955; Prugh *et al.*, 1953; Woodward and Jackson, 1961). Unfortunately, it is not possible from the studies which have examined the benefits of continuing contact with parents to determine how much reduction in distress was due to the visiting *per se*, as the experimental programmes included many other improvements in hospital regime. It should be noted that daily visiting was often associated with tearfulness and distress immediately after the visiting, but that the benefits were shown in the reduced disturbance on the child's return home. It seems that, in early childhood, the presence of familiar family members may be the most important factor in preventing distress following hospitalization.

The evidence that the distress is associated with some kind of interference with attachment behaviour leaves open the question whether the distress arises because separation disrupts an existing bond or because conditions during the separation fail to facilitate attachment behaviour. This has been examined by the Robertsons (1971) who compared the results of short-term fostering (1–2 weeks) in a family setting and in a residential nursery. In both settings the children showed some unhappiness and alteration in behaviour, suggesting that separation as such constituted a stress. On the other hand, marked distress reactions were *only* found in the residential nursery children, which suggested that separation was *not* the most important variable. Unlike the residential nursery, the family fostering provided a continuing intense personal interaction with the *same* individual over time. This is likely to have fostered attachment. Also, however, the family took special steps to maintain the children's bonds with their parents (by keeping to familiar routines, by retaining familiar toys, and by talking about their parents) and it may be that in these circumstances the separation was less likely to disrupt bonds.

At least in young children, distress following hospital admission may be reduced by more personal caretaking in which the child is looked after by the same nurses throughout his hospital stay. In addition, the hospital studies which I have already mentioned suggest that the ill effects following hospital admission may be reduced by attention to ward routines, keeping painful or frightening medical procedures to a minimum, and by providing ample toys and play opportunities. With older children, studies suggest that counselling and other attempts to help them understand their experiences may also be beneficial in preventing disturbances after hospital admission.

Less is known about the ameliorating influences on a child's return home after discharge. However, this is a time when children who have been distressed by their admission tend to be clinging and difficult and it seems highly likely that the parents' response to this behaviour will influence the speed with which the children recover from their experience. Certainly, as already mentioned, the studies with infant rhesus monkeys indicate that the infant's distress after the separation is closely associated with the quality of the parent–infant relationship. The monkey mothers who rejected and rebuffed their clinging offspring were the ones most likely to have disturbed infants. It appears that the mother's behaviour towards her clinging infant after reunion plays an important role in the emotional disturbance. There are no direct studies of a comparable situation with humans, but it seems likely that much the same will occur. Woodward and Jackson (1961) reported that when the mothers of children admitted to a burns unit were helped by a psychiatric social worker to face their own feelings and understand their children's experiences, they were better able to perceive and respond to their children's needs. Children whose mothers had received this counselling showed less emotional disturbance a year after discharge from hospital than did other children admitted to the burns unit. However, as the parental counselling was instituted at the same time as daily visiting it is uncertain which change was mainly responsible for the beneficial results.

(b) *Admission to Hospital: Long-term Effects*

We must turn now to the long-term sequelae of hospital admission. The first point that stands out is that these rarely occur with single hospital admissions, irrespective of the age of the child at the time of admission. On the other hand, *recurrent* hospital admissions (and probably also other kinds of recurrent stressful separation) are associated with an increased risk of psychiatric disorder in later childhood and adolescence. The precise mechanisms which underlie this interesting finding remain uncertain. Two admissions to hospital lasting in total only a few weeks amount to a negligible proportion of the child's life and it is necessary to consider how these brief admissions might lead to long-term psychiatric problems. The crucial data are lacking but the answer may lie in the effects of short-term stress on long-term parent–child interaction. This is suggested by the observation that disorders are more likely to arise when the children come from unhappy or troubled homes (Quinton and Rutter, 1976) and by the animal evidence that the distress following acute separations is in large part a function of disturbances in mother–infant interaction (Hinde and Spencer-Booth, 1970; Hinde and Davies, 1972). Hospital admission in early childhood often leads to clinging and 'difficult' behaviour which interferes with family relationships and it may also sensitize children in such a way that they may be more likely to react adversely next time they go to hospital, which in turn puts a further strain on the family when the child returns home. In this way, although the admissions last only a very short time the disturbed parent–child interaction may last much longer.

That brings us to the other factor, namely chronic stress or disadvantage which has been found to be important in determining whether children have long-term difficulties following hospital admission. In our own studies we found that *chronic* stress increased the likelihood of the occurrence of multiple *acute* stress. Children from homes which were chronically disadvantaged in terms of factors such as marital discord, mental disorder in the mother or serious overcrowding were more likely than other children to have multiple admissions to hospital (Quinton and Rutter). The very fact of multiple admission served as an index of psycho-social disadvantage.

The second way in which chronic disadvantage is important is that it probably increases the children's vulnerability to psychological damage following hospital admission. Our own findings indicated that the association between repeated hospital admission and psychiatric disorder was somewhat stronger in the case of children from disadvantaged homes than it was in the case of youngsters from a more favoured family environment.

5. FAMILY DISCORD

Let us now examine the factors which act as modifying variables in relation to family discord and disharmony. This is the variable to which we have paid most attention in a series of epidemiological family studies. As I have already indicated, there is abundant evidence that children in discordant, unhappy, quarrelsome homes are a group in which the risk of psychiatric disorder in childhood and adolescence is particularly great. Nevertheless, we must not lose perspective. The same studies also indicate that in spite of long-term stress many children in discordant homes do *not* develop psychiatric disorder. Evidence is gradually accumulating on what it is which enables these children to ride the storm and remain on top.

First, there is a variety of studies which suggest an interaction between genetic and environmental variables. In our own investigations we found that the ill effects of marital discord were more marked among children with a mentally ill parent than among children in the general population (although in both groups marital discord was related to child psychiatric disorder). Furthermore, within the group of patients' families, the effects of marital discord were most marked when the parent had a personality disorder, as defined in terms of lifelong handicap (Rutter, 1971; Rutter, Quinton and Yule, in preparation). Of course, while these data certainly suggest some form of interaction effect, they do not necessarily indicate a heredity–environment interaction.

However, adoption studies, in which genetic and non-genetic factors can be differentiated, do point to the possibility of such an interaction with regard to family influences (although marital discord as such has not been examined). For example, Hutchings and Mednick (1974) using a cross-fostering design showed that when the adoptive father was criminal but the biological father was not, the rate of criminality in the offspring was no higher than when neither the biological nor the adoptive father had a crime record. In contrast, when the biological father had a criminal record but the adoptive father did not, there was a twofold increase in criminality in the children. This difference clearly indicates the importance of a genetic effect. On the other hand, the highest rate of criminality in the children was found when *both* the adoptive father and the biological father had a criminal record. In this circumstance the rate of criminality showed a 3½ fold increase. The implication of this finding is that when youngsters have a genetic predisposition to criminality they are more vulnerable to adverse environmental influences in their immediate family—influences which have little impact on children who are not genetically suceptible. Similarly Crowe (1974) investigated 46 children of female offenders who had given up their babies for adoption. The group was compared with an appropriately matched control group. He found that the offspring of the criminal mothers had a much increased rate of definite anti-social personality, in spite of the fact that they had been adopted in infancy. On the other hand, within the group who were presumably genetically vulnerable as a result of having a criminal mother, the development of anti-social problems was related to various adverse experiences in early life. This environmental effect was not found in the control group, again suggesting an interaction between genetic endowment and environmental factors in the development of anti-social personality.

Another kind of interaction was evident in our own data. In a general population study of families of 10-year-old children (Rutter *et al.*, 1975), we identified 6 family variables (including marital discord) all of which were strongly and significantly associated with child psychiatric disorder. We then separated out families which had one, but only one, of any of these risk factors. Thus, in the case of marital discord we identified families with severe marital discord, but *not* low social status, *not* overcrowding, *not* psychiatric disorder in the mother, *not* a criminal father, and in which the child had *not* been taken into care. The very striking finding was that *none* of these risk factors when it occurred in isolation was associated with disorder in the children (Rutter, in preparation). The rate of psychiatric disorder in the children was just the same as in the families without *any* risk factor. In short, even with chronic family stresses the children were not particularly at psychiatric risk if it was really a single stress. However, when any two stresses occurred together the risk went up no less than fourfold. With three and four concurrent stresses the risk went up several times further. It is clear that the combination of chronic stresses provided very much more than an additive effect. There was a striking *interaction* between stress factors which markedly inflated the risk to the child. The risk which attended several concurrent stresses was much more than the sum of the effects of the stresses considered individually. Brown *et al.* (1975) found much the same with vulnerability factors and depression in adults.

These findings all refer to the effects of chronic stresses operating during the same period. What are the implications of a change in family circumstances? To what extent are children better off if family stresses diminish or cease? The first thing that needs to be said in that connection is that longitudinal studies indicate that disadvantages tend to be remarkably persistent (Rutter, 1977). Those children in discordant homes in early childhood are frequently still in discordant homes later in childhood. Nevertheless, things do sometimes change for the better. We studied the effects of improved family circumstances by focusing on children who had all been separated from their parents in earlier childhood as a result of family discord or family problems. Within this group of children who had experienced severe stresses in their earlier life, we compared those who were still in homes characterized by discord and disharmony with those for whom things had improved and who were now in harmonious, happy homes. It was evident that conduct disorders were very much less frequent when discord had ceased. In short, a change for the better in family circumstances was associated with a marked reduction in psychiatric risk for the child.

So far, we have discussed psychiatric risk in terms of differences *between* families. We have concluded that children are most likely to come through stressful experiences unharmed if they are not genetically predisposed, if the stresses are single rather than multiple and if family circumstances improve later in childhood. However, it is also necessary to consider differences *within* families. Even in families where the risk is highest, only some of the children are affected. Why is that? We have looked at this question in several different ways. First of all, we considered children's temperamental characteristics using an approach based on that developed by Thomas, Chess and Birch (1968). We found that children who showed the features of low regularity, low malleability, negative mood, and low fastidiousness were the ones most likely to show psychiatric disorder during the 4-year follow-up period during which we studied the families (Graham, Rutter and George, 1973). Children who had at least 2 of these adverse temperatmental features were 3 times as likely as other children to develop psychiatric problems during the next 4 years (Rutter, Quinton and Yule, in preparation). Interestingly, the temperamental adversity index was more strongly associated with disorders shown during the following 4 years than it was associated with disorders present at the time the child's temperamental features were assessed. In short, it was a true predictor. Why did temperamental adversity put the child at increased risk? Part of the answer is to be found in the effects of parental criti-

cism. Children subjected to frequent criticism by their
parents had a much increased psychiatric risk. But there was
a transactional effect with temperamental adversity. Children
with adverse temperamental characteristics were twice as
likely as other children to be the target of parental criticism.
When parents feel irritable, low, or generally edgy they do
not take it out on all the children to the same extent. It is
a common occurrence for one child to be the butt or scape-
goat. That child is likely to be one whose temperamental
features make him a less easy child to get along with. Thus,
to an appreciable extent, a child's temperament protected
him or put him at risk by virtue of its influence on parent–
child interaction. Even in discordant homes, the temperamen-
tally easy child tended to escape much of the flak.

Our second approach to protective factors was to determine how far one good relationship with a parent protected
a child in an otherwise discordant, unhappy home (Rutter,
1971; Rutter, Quinton and Yule, in preparation). We found
that it provided a quite substantial protective effect. Those
children in discordant homes who had a good relationship
with one parent were much less likely to develop conduct
disorders than children in similar homes who did not have
a good relationship with either parent.

Obviously, it would be important to determine whether
good relationships outside the immediate family could also
serve to have a similar protective effect. Our data do not
allow a really satisfactory answer to that question, but it is
one which warrants further investigation. On the other
hand, we were able to look at the influence of schools.
We found that some schools were much more successful than
others in helping the children to develop normally without
emotional or behavioural problems (Rutter *et al.*, 1975;
Rutter, in preparation; Yule and Rutter, in preparation).
We found that children from disadvantaged and discordant
homes were less likely to develop problems if they attended
better functioning schools. For obvious reasons, this protective effect was most marked in relation to children's behaviour at school. However, it did seem that, to some extent,
good experiences outside the family could mitigate stresses
experienced within the home.

Let me try and draw the threads together. Research findings clearly indicate that many children who experience stress and disadvantage nevertheless achieve emotional security and social competence. As yet, we have only a few scattered findings which enable us to build up a picture of what it is that facilitates this beneficial outcome. In part, it is a question of age-dependent susceptibilities. Children are better able to cope with some forms of stress when they are older than when they are young. There is some suggestion from studies of hospital admission that children can acquire skills which enable them to cope with stress more successfully. Young children who have had experiences of brief, happy, carefully graded separations appear less likely to be damaged by hospital admission in the pre-school years. Presumably, there are similar coping skills which can be acquired in relation to other stresses, although we have yet to identify them. So far as long-term psychological development is concerned, it appears that the great majority of children are well able to cope with single acute stresses without persisting damage. It is recurrent or multiple acute stresses which are most likely to be harmful. Moreover, not only are children from a disadvantaged background or a family with chronic stresses more likely than other children to experience multiple acute stresses, but it is also probable that they are more likely to be *damaged* by such recurrent acute stresses. Interaction effects are also evident in relation to the sequelae of chronic family discord. Children who are especially vulnerable by virtue of their genetic predisposition seem to be those most likely to be damaged by stressful environmental circumstances. As with acute stresses, single, isolated chronic stresses do surprisingly little harm. It is when several stresses occur in combination that the most damage results. However, even in these circumstances children are more likely to develop normally if they have adaptive temperamental characteristics which make them easy to get along with, if they maintain a good relationship with one parent, if family circumstances change for the better and if there are compensating good experiences outside the family, such as at school.

6. PARENTING

Up to this point we have been concerned only with the situations from the child's perspective. However, in clinical practice we usually work with families, and it is important that before concluding we consider why parents behave in the way that they do and how far it is reasonable to expect them to change. This is a large topic and in the limited time available it will be possible to touch on only a few of the main issues. However, these provide some interesting and important parallels with what has already been discussed in relation to children.

(a) *Childhood Experiences*

In part, parents are what they are because of their own experiences in childhood and earlier life. There are now a number of studies which have shown that individuals reared in unhappy, discordant, disrupted homes are more likely when adult to marry in their teens, to have illegitimate children, to have unhappy marriages and to have difficulties in child rearing (see review by Rutter and Madge, 1976). The most serious disorders of parenting, as reflected in child battering, are particularly likely to follow very bad experiences in childhood. In part, people care for their children in the way that they do because of the way they themselves were brought up. We know that these links between childhood experiences and parenting behaviour are far from inevitable. Many individuals who have had terrible experiences in childhood nevertheless become perfectly adequate parents. However, we know very little about the factors that enable them to be so nor do we have much information in humans about the extent to which serious abnormalities in parenting are reversible. On the other hand, the findings from animal studies are encouraging. One of the striking observations in Harlow's studies (1958; Harlow and Harlow, 1969), of rhesus monkeys subjected to extreme social isolation in infancy, was the devestating effect that these early experiences had on later sexual and maternal behaviour. The deprived female monkeys were often severely rejecting of their offspring and sometimes killed them. What is interesting and important in this connection is that the further studies of these same monkeys have shown that many of the isolated monkeys were considerably better mothers for their second infant (Harlow and Suomi, 1971). Research is beginning to delineate what are the factors needed for this improvement in parenting function to take place (Suomi and Harlow, 1972; Suomi, 1973; Novak and Harlow, 1975). Of course, we must be very careful in drawing parallels between animal behaviour and human behaviour but the implication seems to be that even in adult life, individuals who have been severely damaged by early life experiences can still show marked and worthwhile improvements in their behaviour. The very limited evidence from human studies is in accord with this conclusion.

(b) *Experience of Child Rearing*

In this context it is relevant to note that several human studies have shown that parents interact very differently with their second child compared with the way they dealt with their first (see Rutter and Madge, 1976). Parents are, of course, inexperienced with their firstborn and are naturally anxious and uncertain in their handling. The findings indicate the appreciable modifiability of parental behaviour as shown by the different handling of the second child. Parents are influenced in how they behave by the characteristics of their children and by the very experience of child rearing. This effect has already been discussed in relation to children's temperamental characteristics. Another example is provided by follow-up studies of children born after their mothers have applied for an abortion and been refused. This is a group of children who were unplanned, unwanted and rejected, as evidenced by their mothers' attempts to destroy them before birth. Not surprisingly, children born after this unpromising start do have rather more difficulties in later development than other children (Forssman and Thuwe, 1966). However, what is equally striking is the high proportion of mothers who subsequently develop positive feelings and good relationships towards their children, and the relatively high proportion of the children who develop normally in spite of their bad start (Dytrych *et al.* 1975).

(c) *Mental Disorder, Marital Discord and Parent–Child Interaction*

If we turn now to how parent–child interaction is influenced by the current family situation, we find a complex interaction between mental disorder, marital discord and disturbed parent–child relationships (Quinton, Rutter, and Rowlands, 1977; Rutter, Quinton, and Yule, in preparation). The close association between psychiatric disorder in adult life and marital disharmony has already been noted. The interaction is probably two-way; that is marital problems predispose to the development of neurotic disturbance, and also depression and emotional disorder increase the likelihood of disturbed relationships between husband and wife. Both these situations are in turn associated with problems in parenting. Mental disorder impairs family functioning and interferes with parent–child relationships. Similarly, when parents quarrel and show hostility, the children are often drawn into the dispute and suffer accordingly. It may be concluded that if parents are to be helped in caring for their children, attention needs to be paid both to their mental health and to their marital relationship.

(d) *Social Circumstances*

However, family circumstances cannot be considered in isolation from the wider social environment. Our comparative studies of inner London and the Isle of Wight (Rutter, Yule *et al.*, 1975) show that working-class women in the Metropolis are particularly vulnerable to psychiatric disorder, especially depression. This is not just a function of low social status, as the social class relationship was not found on the Isle of Wight. Rather it is a combination of low social status and the particular living conditions found in inner city areas. In this connection, it should be noted that the association is with *current* social conditions and not with the social circumstances into which the parent was *born*. We do not know exactly what it is about inner city life which causes the stress for working-class women, but the implication is that if these stresses could be diminished, their mental health would improve and that this might well have benefits for the children.

As a society, we are constantly exhorting parents to do better and the bookshops are full of books on how parents should bring up their children. Unfortunately, less attention has been paid to what needs to be done to help parents improve their family functioning. Some leads are available, as I have indicated, but further research and greater knowledge are required if we are going to be in a really sound position to help parents to be better able to help themselves.

7. CONCLUSIONS

There is a tendency in some quarters at the moment to look at the future with gloom. People point to the figures which indicate a rising divorce rate, rising illegitimacy ratio, an increasing proportion of births to teenage mothers, an increasing number of one-parent families, and a delinquency rate which gets greater every year (see Rutter and Madge, 1976). All these trends are real and of course they are a serious cause for concern, but I think there are also reasons for optimism as I hope has been implicit in all that I have said. Development is fluid and it is never too late for changes to take place. Even with the worst circumstances that human beings can devise only a porportion of the children succumb, and ameliorating factors can do much to aid normal development. There is a widening—although still limited—knowledge of how children and parents can overcome stresses and disadvantage. If we can increase our understanding of these influences and harness the knowledge already available to our policies and to our patterns of treatment, perhaps something useful can be achieved. Of course, we shall not eliminate suffering. Nevertheless some children who would otherwise have succumbed may be helped to survive stressful circumstances and to develop emotional security and social competence.

REFERENCES

AINSWORTH, M. D. S., *Infancy in Uganda: Infant Care and Growth of Love*. Baltimore: Johns Hopkins Press, 1967.

AINSWORTH, M. D. S., BELL, S. M. and STAYTON, D. J., 'Individual differences in strange-situation behaviour of one-year-olds.' In H. A. Schaffer (ed.), *The Origins of Human Social Relations*, London: Academic Press, 1971.

ARSENIAN, J. M., 'Young children in an insecure situation.' *Journal of Abnormal and Social Psychology*, 38, 225–43, 1943.

BOWLBY, J., *Attachment and Loss: Vol. 1. Attachment*. London: Hogarth Press, 1969.

BOWLBY, J., *Attachment and Loss: Vol. 2. Separation: Anxiety and Anger*. Harmondsworth: Penguin, 1975.

BROWN, G. W., BHROLCHAIN, M. and HARRIS, T. 'Social class and psychiatric disturbance among women in an urban population'. *Sociology*, 9, 225–54, 1975.

COWEN, E. L., PEDERSON, A., BABIGION, H., IZZO, L. D. and TROST, M. A., 'Long-term follow-up of early detached vulnerable children.' *Journal of Consulting and Clinical Psychology*, 41, 438–46, 1973.

COATES, B., ANDERSON, E. P. and HARTUP, W. W., 'The stability of attachment behaviours in the human infant.' *Development Psychology*, 6, 231–7, 1972.

COHEN, L. J., 'The operational definition of human attachment.' *Psychological Bulletin*, 81, 107–217, 1974.

COHEN, L. J. and CAMPOS, J. J., 'Father, mother, and stranger as elicitors of attachment behaviours in infancy.' *Development Psychology*, 10, 146–54, 1974.

CROWE, R. R., 'An adoption study of antisocial personality.' *Archives of General Psychiatry*, 31, 785–91, 1974.

DOUGLAS, J. W. B., 'Early hospital admissions and later disturbances of behaviour and learning.' *Developmental Medicine and Child Neurology*, 17, 456–80, 1975.

DYTRYCH, Z. MATERJCEK, U., SCHULLER, V., DAVID, H. P. and FRIEDMAN, H. L. Children born to women denied abortion. *Family Planning Perspectives*, 7, 165–171, 1975.

FAGIN, C. N. R. N., *The Effects of Maternal Attendance During Hospitalization on the Post-Hospital Behavior of Young Children: A Comparative Study*. Philadelphia: F. A. Davies, 1966.

FAUST, O. A., JACKSON, K., CERMACK, E. G., BURTT, M. M. and WINKLEY, R., *Reducing Emotional Trauma in Hospitalized Children*. Albany Research Project, Albany, New York, 1952. (Cited in Yarrow, L. J., 1964.)

FORSSMAN, J. and THUWE, I., 'One hundred and twenty children born after application for theraputic abortion refused.' *Acta Psychiatrica Scandinavica*, 42, 71–88, 1966.

GRAHAM, P., RUTTER, M. and GEORGE, S., 'Temperamental characteristics as predictors of behaviour disorders in children.' *American Journal of Orthopsychiatry*, 43, 328–39, 1973.

HARLOW, H. F., 'The nature of love.' *American Psychologist*, 13, 673–85, 1958.

HARLOW, H. F. and HARLOW, M. K., 'Effects of various mother-infant relationships on rhesus monkey behaviours.' In B. M. Foss (ed.), *Determinants of Infant Behaviour, Vol. 4*, London: Methuen, 1969.

HARLOW, H. F. and SUOMI, S. J., 'Social recovery by isolation-reared monkeys.' *Proceedings of the National Academy of Sciences*, 68, 1534–8, 1971.

HARLOW, H. F. and ZIMMERMAN, R. R., 'Affectional responses in the infant monkey.' *Science*, 130, 421–32, 1959.

HEINICKE, C. M. and WESTHEIMER, I. J., *Brief Separations*. London: Longmans, 1965.

HINDE, R. A. and DAVIES, L., 'Removing infant rhesus from mother for 13 days compared with removing mother from infant.' *Journal of Child Psychology and Psychiatry*, 13, 227–37, 1972.

HINDE, R. A. and SPENCER-BOOTH, Y., 'Individual differences in the responses of rhesus monkeys to a period of separation from their mothers.' *Journal of Child Psychology and Psychiatry*, 11, 159–76, 1970.

HUTCHINGS, B. and MEDNICK, S. A., 'Registered criminality in the adoptive and biological parents of registered male adoptees.' In S. A. Mednick *et al.* (eds.), *Genetics, Environment and Psychopathology*, Amsterdam: North Holland, 215–27, 1974.

ILLINGWORTH, R. S. and HOLT, K. S., 'Children in hospital: some observations on their reactions with special reference to daily visiting.' *Lancet*, 2, 1257–62, 1955.

KISSEL, S., 'Stress-reducing properties of social stimuli.' *Journal of Personality and Social Psychology*, 2, 378–84, 1965.

MACCOBY, E. E. and FELDMAN, S. S., 'Mother-attachment and stranger reactions in the third year of life. *Monographs of the Society for Reserach in Child Development*, 37, Serial number 146, 1972.

MACCOBY, E. E. and MASTERS, J. C., 'Attachment and dependency.' In P. Mussen (ed.), *Carmichael's Manual of Child Psychology*, 3rd edition, New York: Wiley, 1970.

McCORD, W. and McCORD, J., *Origins of Crime: A New Evaluation of the Cambridge-Somerville Youth Study.* New York: Columbia University Press, 1959.

MASON, W. A. and KENNEY, M. D., 'Redirection of filial attachments in rhesus monkeys: dogs as mother surrogates.' *Science*, 183, 1209–11, 1974.

MASTERS, J. C. and WELLMAN, H. M., 'The study of human infant attachment: a procedural critique.' *Psychological Bulletin*, 81, 218–37, 1974.

NOVAK, M. A. and HARLOW, H. F., 'Social recovery of monkeys isolated for the first year of life. 1. Rehabilitation and therapy.' *Developmental Psychology*, 11, 453–65, 1975.

POWER, M., ASH, P., SHOENBERG, E. and SIREY, C., 'Delinquency and the family.' *British Journal of Social Work*, 4, 13–38, 1974.

PRUGH, D. G., STAUB, E.M., SANDS, H. H., KIRSHBAUM, R. M. and LENIHAN, E. A., 'A study of the emotional reactions of children and families to hospitalization and illness.' *Amercian Journal of Orthopsychiatry*, 23, 70–106, 1953.

QUINTON, D. and RUTTER, N., 'Early hospital admissions and later disturbances of behaviour: an attempted replication of Douglas' findings.' *Development Medicine and Child Neurology*, 18, 447–59, 1976.

QUINTON, D., RUTTER, M. and ROWLANDS, O., 'An evaluation of·
an interview assessment of marriage.' *Psychological Medicine,* 6,
577–86, 1976.
ROBERTSON, J. and ROBERTSON, J., 'Young children in brief sep-
arations: a fresh look.' *Psychoanalytic Study of the Child,* 26,
264-315, 1971.
ROFF, M., SELLS, S. B. and GOLDEN, M. M., *Social Adjustment and
Personality Development in Children.* Minneapolis: University of
Minnesota Press, 1972.
ROSENTHAL, M. K., 'Attachment and mother–infant interaction:
some research impasses and a suggested change in orientation.'
Journal of Child Psychology and Psychiatry, 14, 201-8, 1973.
RUTTER, M., 'Parent–child separation: psychological effects on the
children.' *Journal of Child Psychology and Psychiatry,* 12, 233-60,
1971.
RUTTER, M., *Maternal Deprivation Reassessed.* Harmondsworth:
Penguin, 1972.
RUTTER, M. (ed.), *The Child, His Family and the Community.* Lon-
don: Wiley, in preparation.
RUTTER, M., 'Prospective studies to investigate behavioural change.'
In J. S. Strauss, H. M. Babigian and M. Roff (eds.), *Methods of
Longitudinal Research in Psychopathology,* New York: Plenum,
1977.
RUTTER, M., GRAHAM, P., CHADWICK, O., and YULE, W., 'Ado-
lescent turmoil: fact or fiction.' *Journal of Child Psychology and
Psychiatry,* 17, 35-56, 1976.
RUTTER, M. and MADGE, N., *Cycles of Disadvantage.* London: Heine-
mann Educ., 1976.
RUTTER, M. and QUINTON, D., 'Psychiatric disorder—ecological fac-
tors and concept of causation.' In H. McGurk (ed.), *Ecological Fac-
tors in Human Development,* Amsterdam: North Holland, 1977.
RUTTER, M., QUINTON, D., and YULE, W., *Family Pathology and
Disorder in Children.* London: Wiley, in preparation.
RUTTER, M., TIZARD, J., and WHITMORE, K. (eds.), *Education,
Health and Behaviour.* London: Longman, 1970.
RUTTER, M., YULE, B., QUINTON, D., ROWLANDS, O., YULE, W.,
and BERGER, M., 'Attainment and adjustment in two geographical
areas: III. Some factors accounting for area differences.' *British
Journal of Psychiatry,* 126, 520-33, 1975.
SCHAFFER, H. R. and EMERSON, P. E., 'The development of social
attachments in infancy.' *Monographs of the Society for Research in
Child Development,* 19, 3, 1-77, 1964.
SCHWARTZ, J., 'Effects of peer familiarity on the behaviour of pre-
schoolers in a novel situation.' *Journal of Personality and Social
Psychology,* 24, 276-84, 1972.
SHIELDS, J., 'Polygenic influences.' In M. Rutter and L. Hersov (eds.),
Child Psychiatry: Modern Approaches, London: Blackwell Scientific,
1977.

SPELKE, E., ZELAZO, P., KAGAN, J., and KOTELCHOCK, M., 'Father interaction and separation protest.' *Developmental Psychology*, 9, 83–90, 1973.
STACEY, M., DREARDEN, R., PILL, R., and ROBINSON, D., *Hospitals, Children and their Families: The Report of a Pilot Study*. London: Routledge and Kegan Paul, 1970.
STAYTON, D. J. and AINSWORTH, M. D. S., 'Individual differences in infant responses to brief, everyday separations as related to other infant and maternal behaviours.' *Developmental Psychology*, 9, 226–35, 1973.
STAYTON, D. J., AINSWORTH, M. D. S., and MAIN, D. B., 'The development of separation behaviour in the first year of life: protest, following and greeting.' *Developmental Psychology*, 9, 213–25, 1973.
STEVENS, A., 'Attachment and polymetric rearing.' Thesis for D.M., University of Oxford, 1975.
SUNDBY, H. S. and KREYBERG, P. C., *Prognosis in Child Psychiatry*. Baltimore: Williams and Wilkins, 1969.
SUOMI, S. J., 'Surrogate rehabilitation of monkeys reared in total social isolation.' *Journal of Child Psychology*, 14, 71–7, 1973.
SUOMI, S. J. and HARLOW, H. F., 'Social rehabilitation of isolate-reared monkeys.' *Developmental Psychology*, 6, 487–96, 1972.
TIZARD, J. and REES, J., 'The effect of early institutional rearing on the behaviour problems and affectional relationships of four-year-old children.' *Journal of Child Psychology and Psychiatry*, 16, 61–74, 1975.
THOMAS, A., CHESS, S., and BIRCH, H. G., *Temperament and Behavior Disorders in Children*. New York: University Press, 1968.
VERNON, D. T. A., FOLEY, J. M.,SIPOWICZ, R. R.,and SCHULMAN, J. L., *The Psychological Responses of Children to Hospitalization and Illness*. Springfield, Ill.: Chas. C. Thomas, 1965.
VERNON, D. T. A., FOLEY, J. M., and SCHULMAN, J. L., 'Effect of mother–child separation and birth order on young children's responses to two potentially stressful experiences.' *Journal of Personality and Social Psychology*, 5, 162–74, 1967.
WEST, D. J. and FARRINGTON, D. P., *Who Becomes Delinquent?* London: Heinemann, 1973.
WOODWARD, J. and JACKSON, D., 'Emotional reactions in burned children and their mothers.' *British Journal of Plastic Surgery*, 13, 316–24, 1961.
YARROW, L. J., 'Separation from parents during early childhood.' In M. L. Hoffman and L. W. Hofman (eds.), *Review of Child Development Research, Vol. 1*, New York: Russell Sage Foundation, 1964.
YULE, B. and RUTTER, M., In preparation.
ZAX, M., COWEN, E. L., RAPPAPORT, J., BEACH, D. R., and LAIRD, J. D., 'Follow-up study of children identified as emotionally disturbed.' *Journal of Consulting and Clinical Psychology*, 32, 369–74, 1968.

3 Learning How To Do Things With Words

JEROME BRUNER

I have had a share of good fortune in having been in attendance at the two preceding Wolfson Lectures in the series. Both of these lectures had the effect of altering the plans I had made for my own lecture—a somewhat unsettling if exhilarating experience. But it has provided me with an opportunity to reconsider the nature of language development from the different perspectives provided by my colleagues. I shall begin, then, by setting my own task, but before going on, I would like to double back over some of the major themes from earlier lectures, better to relate to them.

What I shall be discussing is how the human infant learns to use language in a fashion that meets the requirements of social living, as a member of a culture-using species. To succeed at such living requires far more than that one speak in well-formed sentences, or that one's words and sentences meet the requirements of reference and meaning and truth-testability. To speak, rather, requires that one's utterances meet criteria of conventional appropriateness or felicity not only with respect to the context in which speech occurs, but also to the acts of those with whom one is involved in dialogue. If I say 'Italy is a boot', the sentence may be well formed, but it is quite unclear whether it is true or false, useful or useless, appropriate or inappropriate unless you know to whom it is addressed and under what circumstances. To anyone conversant with the debates in linguistics and linguistic philosophy over the last fifteen years—ever since

John Austin first introduced these matters—this will all have a very common-sense and familiar ring. But I should like to probe a bit further. I would like to explore in a more system-atic empirical way how communicative functions are actually realized in the life of very young children and how the nature of early interaction between mother and child provides the matrix for the acquisition of language and, indeed, gives it its distinctive structure. Once one examines the detail of early language acquisition, how the child goes from prelin-guistic communication to the early mastery of language, it will come as no surprise that, later, the question 'How would you feel about a breath of fresh air?' is not interpreted as inquiring into one's naïve theory of respiratory physiology but as an invitation to go for a walk.

Now let me double back briefly. The two previous speak-ers, considering the development of the child, have stressed the powerful role of interaction, of skills in maintaining a connection with adults and peers. Professor Hinde's emphasis was upon the structure of a primate group and how it affec-ted the attachment of the young macaques he was investi-gting. For Professor Rutter, the establishment and mainten-ance of social connection was proposed as the buffering factor that prevented a poor family-social background from pressuring a child into an abnormal pattern of development. My own lecture will be in the same spirit, and I shall be emphasizing, as I noted, the manner in which the child's transition from his primate background into the use of the powerful cultural tool of language depends upon the develop-ment and, indeed, the exploitation of the mother–infant bond.

1. MODELS OF LANGUAGE ACQUISITION

I must now intone a necrology in order to set the back-ground. It is for LAD, Chomsky's (1962) famous Language Acquisition Device, a veritable child prodigy that, for its ten years of sway, helped produce a new way of seeing what is involved in acquiring language—and thereby dug its own grave. LAD, for those not acquainted with it, was what lin-guists refer to as a discovery procedure, that is to say, a means of discovering the rules by which acceptable sentences in a language are put together. Its input was a sample of the

owever encountered; its output was the set of
rules that would generate all the well-formed
possible in the language and none that were ill-
he base of this recognition or discovery programme
was presumed to be the language-learner's innate grasp of the
universals of language. The local language being learned,
according to this view, was merely a realization in local form
of the syntatic universals of language. The innate grasp of
these linguistic universals of language was assumed to be independent of any knowledge of the non-linguistic world. Nor,
indeed, did the recognition programme require anything
more than that the learner (or discoverer) of the language be
a bystander: the spoken corpus of speech flowed round and
into him, and the rules came out the other end. It did not
require, for example, that he should already know what the
language referred to—that he should have concepts about the
real world being referred to—nor that the learner should have
to enter into particular kinds of dialogue with the speakers
of the language. As an enthusiastic David McNeill put it in
1970, 'The facts of language acquisition could not be as they
are unless the concept of a sentence is available to children
at the start of their learning.'

A decent necrologist should not carp. There are some
features of LAD that are plainly and baldly wrong. The
child's knowledge of language is deeply dependent upon a
prior mastery of concepts about the world to which language will refer. Those of you who had the good fortune to
hear Dr. Eve Clark's paper in this series of lectures will appre-
ciate to what degree this point is buttressed by data. It is
also clear, and will hopefully be clearer before the hour is
out, how dependent language acquisition is upon the nature
of the interaction that takes place between child and mother.
Being a witness at the feast of language is not enough of an
exposure to assure acquisition. There must be contingent
interaction. But for all that, Chomsky has taught us something that is profoundly important. It is that the child is
equipped with some means for generating hypotheses about
language that could not simply be the result of learning by
association and reinforcement what words go with what
in the presence of what things. There is indeed something

pre-programmed about our language-acquiring capacity. But we need not, as my good friend George Miller once put it, vacillate between an impossible theory that assumes we learn everything by association (the facts deny it and the sheer arithmetic tells us that there would be just too much to learn even in a dozen lifetimes), and, on the other hand, a magical theory that says we already know about sentences before we start. There appears to be some readiness, rather, quickly to grasp certain rules for forming sentences, once we know what the world is about to which the sentences refer. And the rules that govern these sentences are neither imitated—for often one does not find them in the speech of the adults with whom the child is in contact—nor are they to be thought of as simple reflections of the world of concepts that the child has learned for dealing with the extra-linguistic environment, though they are plainly related. So though we come to bury LAD, we must not be so foolish as to withhold all praise.

I should like to propose an alternative. I shall propose that the child communicates before he has language. He does so in order to carry out certain functions that are vital to the species. These primitive communicative acts are effected by gesture, vocalization, and the exploitation of context. There is enough that is universal about such pre-lexico-grammatical communication to suggest that a part of it is innate, and easily triggered. There is a progressive development of these primitive procedures for communicating, and typically they are replaced by less primitive ones until eventually they are replaced by standard linguistic procedures. These progressive changes and procedural leaps are massively dependent upon the interaction of the mother (a word I shall use for 'caretaker' generally with a certain statistical licence) and the child. Mothers *teach* their children to speak, however willing the children may be, and I rather take their willingness to be part of the innate preparation for language. Washoe and Sarah and the other talking chimps (Brown, 1973), viewed closely, are *not* eager pupils.

The progressive changes that occur prelinguistically seem to provide precursors or, to use the stronger word, prerequisites for mastering lexico-grammatical speech. Concerned as I shall be this evening with the growth of reference and with the emergence of communication in support of joint action, I shall sketch roughly what I think may be involved in such development.

With respect to reference, it would seem that at the start there is a strong push present in the infant to share features of the sensory world with the mother and an equally strong push for the mother to orient to the features of the world to which the child is attending. At the outset, referential activity on the part of the child is very much captive of his needs: he tends to attend to what he wants and to show signs of wanting it. He has intentions and shows them, gesturally and vocally and in appropriate contexts. Mothers invariably interpret signs of desire as intentional communicative acts, and respond appropriately. As Ainsworth and Bell (1974) have shown, the mothers who respond to their children's vocalization during the first half of the first year end up in the last quarter of that year with children who cry less and vocalize and gesture more in a communicative way. In time, the sharing of attention is extended by both parties to matters that are sensorially vivid, or surprising or even rare. Indexing procedures, gestural and vocal, emerge and change. They very rarely have the character of being signs for specific events, but, as Harrison (1972) notes, they are procedures for noting which among several candidates for attention has in fact achieved the focus of attention—reaching toward, pointing, etc. Betimes, as the child develops models of what constitutes a steady-state environment, he begins to develop means of indicating objects and events that diverge from his theory or model of that world. It is interesting that a profound change in his signalling occurs at this point. And at the end of the first year there emerges yet another distinct step: the deep hypothesis that how one vocalizes affects how another's attention can be altered, that sounds and sound patterns have semanticity. At that point, a quite new means of generating hypotheses, strongly influenced by mother's utterances, comes into being. Something more like the philosopher's reference and less like ostension emerges. We shall see more of this in a moment.

With respect to action and joint action, let me sketch

briefly what is at issue. For anybody to understand action, whether he be child or adult, requires the ability to categorize a flow of events in a complex, possibly natural way. Most human action has at least the following minimal set of categorizable components: the act itself, an agent, an object, a recipient of the action, an instrument, a locus, and a time marker. Or to say it in common sense, understanding the actions of human beings involves knowing what is done to what, by whom, to whom, where, by what instrument, and in what order. It is also necessary to distinguish its start and its finish. All of that is obvious, and I even suggested that it was 'natural', a moot point. In order to communicate in a way that makes possible joint action, there must be, at very least, some way of signalling the intent to act as well as indicating when one's intentions have been fulfilled, but that is scarcely enough for regulation. There must also be a way of indicating what the action is, who is to be the agent and who the recipient, on what object is the action to be performed and with what instrument, where and when. You will immediately recognize my list as being a parallel to the classic case grammar with categories like subject, verb, object, indirect object, locative, instrumentive, plus some form of time or tense marker. There must, as well, be some primitive mood marking procedure to distinguish indicating from commanding or requesting. For full effectiveness, there must be also some way of using these cases in a rule-bound order in an utterance that permits shifting and substitutability. For now I am the agent and you the recipient, and then you become the agent and I the recipient, and sometimes you use the instrument in a particular place, and sometimes I do but in a different place. And to be effective in signalling about the course of an action, I must be able to indicate when something should start and when it should stop—and not just the action as a whole, but those parts of it that are carried by an agent or recipient, are directed to particular objects with particular instruments, etc.

By this recounting of the obvious, I hope I have convinced you of three things. The first is that the course of action is nicely matched to the structure of speech: that the two are not arbitrarily related. The second is that it takes a fair amount of early learning to master the intricacies of joint action, even without language proper. And the third is that the conventions and procedures by which we represent the aspects of action—case grammar—do not naturally arise out of our mastery of joint action in and of itself, although a knowledge of the requirements of joint action would surely provide some powerful hints to the learner about the structure of the linguistic code. And perhaps there is a fourth matter of which you may have become convinced: that for human beings to share in an action, with or without the aid of regulatory language, there must be a considerable amount of intersubjective sharing between them, a sharing of many presuppositions that buffer the co-operating parties from shocked surprise—the classic problem of 'other minds'.

2. JOINT ATTENTION AND REFERENCE

We come now to the empirical part of our inquiry. We have been studying children from roughly three months of age to about their second birthday, visiting them in their homes fortnightly, and video-recording a half-hour of ordinary play-interaction between the mother and child, often much enriched by the presence of the experimenter. This has been supplemented by occasional video-recordings made by parents of behaviour they thought we should see and had not (often very valuable indeed) and by diary records. As a preliminary, we looked at six children in this way; more latterly we have concentrated on three, and I shall mostly be telling you about two of them. The object of the exercise was to explore how communication between the pairs was established before language proper came on the scene and how, gradually, the older modes of communication were replaced by more standard language. Our effort, as you may guess from what has already been said, was to explore how language was used, how its forms were made to serve functions. I shall concentrate as noted on two uses of communication: for referring and for carrying out joint action. I choose the two because they may stem from quite different roots, the one relating to the sharing of attention, the other to the management of complementary intentions. In each of them we shall see the emergence of communicative forms that have language-like properties which, at the opportune moment, and with the help of an adult, provide a clue for the child as to how to crack the linguistic code he is encountering. Let me say, before turning to these matters, that I shall not burden you with the dates or milestones at which new forms appear in language, but only with rough indications. It is the order of emergence that matters rather than absolute dates, for some children learn quickly and some less so, with no seeming effect on later performance. Nor is it evident that all children go through precisely the same order, for the literature on the subject and our own data suggest that order is dependent on context in some degree and reflects the individual progress of the mother–infant bond.

So let me turn first to the course of reference. The deep question about reference is how one individual manages to get another to share, attend to, zero in upon a topic that is occupying him. At the start, the child can neither reach nor point toward an object that he wants or is interested in. He can of course cry or fret, he can of course look at what interests him and that, as we shall see, stands him in good stead. As for the mother, her options are almost as limited as the child's: neither her vocalizations nor her gestures are able to accomplish the end of bringing the child's attention to objects or events she wishes to single out. From the mother's side, her first and most useful basis for sharing the child's 'referent' is her power of interference backed by her inevitable theory of what the child is intending. She inevitably interprets the child's actions as related to wants and needs: he cries because he is hungry or wet, stares at something because he wants to take possession of it or, simply, is 'fascinated by it'. She is not the least disturbed by the difficulty of philosophers in establishing communicative intent, how we know that others are attempting to send a message. She simply assumes it, and indeed, Macfarlane's (1974) study of greeting rituals of mothers toward their newborns suggests that, from the start, the maternal theory is premised on the infant's acts being purposeful and his gestures and vocalizations being attempted communications. It is not surprising, then, that in a recent study by Collis and Schaffer (1975), the mother's line of regard follows the infant's line of regard virtually all the time that the two of them are together in an undistracted situation. But perhaps more interesting is the infant's behaviour. Dr. Michael Scaife (Scaife and Bruner, 1975) working in my laboratory here at Oxford has demonstrated that infants as young as four months of age will also follow the mother's line of regard outward to the surrounding environment. Some of you who have read about infantile egocentrism may be surprised, since this indicates that the child can use another axis than his own egocentric one to guide his orientation. Scaife now reports that there are indications that such gaze-following may occur even when the child is not interacting directly with the adult involved. If two adults, conversing with each other, now look jointly in a convergent direction, and they are within the infant's range of attention, the infant's line of regard will often converge with theirs, all of this before the infant is much over a year.

Before the child begins his reaching career, his chief focus of attention is his mother's face, eye contact leading to smiles, vocalizations, and a variety of exchange manœuvres— of which more later. Once the child begins reaching for objects, however, *en face* contact between mother and child drops drastically from about 80 per cent of contact time to roughly 15 per cent. Characteristically at this stage the child either orients to the objects he reaches for, manipulates, and mouths, *or* he orients to the mother. At 5 months, for example, he never looks to the mother when his attempts to reach or to grasp an object fail. He is possessed by the one or the other and does not alternate. At this stage, the chief communicative feature of the child's object-directed activity is his first vocalization in the event of not being able to reach or get hold of something he wants.

Note the infant's typical reach at this stage. It is an effortful gesture reeking with intention to possess the object: hand and arm fully extended, fist opening and closing, body bent forward, mouth often working, eyes fixed on the object. This gestural effort, which gives no indication of being communicatively directed toward the mother, is none the less treated by her as communicatively intended, and the mother often obtains an object the child cannot reach. The child in time comes to expect this support.

By 8 months, usually, the child's reach metamorphoses. It becomes markedly less exigent, and he begins looking toward the mother while he is in the act of reaching for an object. The gesture is changing from an instrumental reach to something more like an indicator—a semi-extended arm, hand held somewhat angled upward, fingers no longer in grasp position, body no longer stretched fully forward. His gaze shifts from object to mother and back. He can now reach-for-real and reach-to-signal.

For a few months after the appearance of indicative reaching, there is a transitional phase. Indicative reaching becomes dissociated from the intention to get an object: it may signal only and the child may not even take an indicated object that is proffered. Indicative reaching increasingly extends outward to objects more remote spatially. And, characteristically, the mother conforms to the change, interpreting reaching as interest rather than as desire, and chatting accordingly to the child's reach.

What emerges next suggests that new forms of communication emerge initially to fulfil old functions, and then bring in new functions with them. It is the pure point, and in no sense is it gesturally like a reach—forefinger extended, the infant not reaching bodily forward. Initially it is used like an indicating reach. But like most new forms, pointing explodes in usage soon after first appearance. At 13 months, for example, six pure points were observed in Richard in a half-hour's play with his mother. At 14 months/3 weeks, in a holiday setting, 29 pure points occurred in the same time, and in a three-hour observation session the next day more than a hundred were observed. The objects selected as targets were governed by the following rules: (a) objects more than a metre distant and either novel or in an unexpected context, (b) neither novel nor unexpected, but a *picture* of a familiar object, (c) neither novel nor pictured, but imaginary or hypothetical, the locus being indicated (as pointing upward to the ceiling, and saying 'bird'). Though Richard had few words, he was working on the hypothesis that his uttered sounds had semanticity. And we should note, finally, that his pointing was typically accompanied by vocalization and by looking back at the interlocutor. Needless to say, his mother interprets his pointing much as she would interpret that of an adult.

I should like to note one thing particularly about the growth of pointing over the next months. It is extended to many things, as in indicating a choice between objects, aiding request, and so on. But it is also a prime instrument in the children we have studied for exploring the relation between objects and both their loci and possessors. At 15½ months, the turning on of a light evokes in Richard a point toward the ceiling and 'li(ght)'; later the sound of an auto in the drive produces a point toward it and 'Daddy'; a picture of a wine bottle in a book results in a point to the bare dining table, etc. Such instances are invariably shared by glancing back at the adult. I mention this point here to make clear one matter that tends to be swamped by the implicit notion that referencing or indexing is somehow associative. I would urge that however associative it may be, such indicating behaviour also serves for generating and testing hypotheses, bringing objects (even if they are hypothetical) into the realm of discourse.

Again, the mother goes readily along with the new development and begins incorporating the child's pointing and his interest in semantic or naming sounds into dialogue. Indeed, it was the Russian linguist Shvachkin (1948) who noted that the child's interest in the phonemic system of the language coincided with his interest in naming. The mother's new medium for dialogue is 'book reading', and I have no doubt that cultures without picture books find suitable substitutes.

Looking at picture books together concentrates the joint attention of mother and infant upon highly compressed foci of attention.* They are foci of attention, moreover, that by virtue of being representations rather than real things eliminate competition from virtually all other response systems— notably the reaching system. In this sense, the medium is part of the message and it is not surprising that, at the earliest stage, the mother spends hard effort in getting the

*The work on 'book-reading' has been done jointly with Dr. Anat Ninio of The Hebrew University of Jerusalem.

child into the medium—converting the book from an object to be banged and mauled into a carrier of pictures to be looked at. The end point of that enterprise is the establishment of a dialogue pattern, and that dialogue pattern, we shall see, is crucial to the development of labelling.

There is a period of several months—from a year to about fifteen months—when the mother's strategy seems to be devoted to getting the child to look, to point, and to vocalize at the right junctures in the dialogue exchanges between them. I fully agree with Catherine Snow (in press) that the establishment of such turn-taking, sequenced dialogue is a prerequisite for language acquisition. In Richard's case, the dialogue is controlled by three linguistic devices used by his mother in a highly predictable way. The first is the attentional vocative *Look* or some variant, appropriately accompanied by pointing. The second is what linguists call a 'Wh.. question' and it takes the form of some such question as 'What's that, Richard?' again often with a supporting point. Interrogatives are not novel: they constitute from a third to a half of the mother's utterances during the first year, a matter to which we shall return. The third device is labelling. During this stage and the next, described later, the mother's labels are always nominals—object words or proper names, never attributes or states or actions.

The dialogue exchanges initiated by one mother while she and Richard were looking at pictures together show the following striking regularity. Where there are two or more rounds in the exchange, in eight cases out of ten, the mother says 'Look' before either asking a 'Wh.. question' or proferring a label. If there are only 'Wh.. questions' and labels in the dialogue, the former precede the latter. The almost invariant order was from a vocative through a question to a realization of the label. And each was given in an appropriate context. And so, for example, 'Wh.. questions' follow only upon the child's gesture of pointing, and never upon a vocalization. A wide range of vocalizations are accepted in this first 'dialogue establishing' stage as appropriate responses to either an attentional vocative or a 'Wh.. question', however wide they may be of the standard lexical mark. If Richard responds with a vocalization, his mother's response to him in the great majority of cases is a label. Indeed, in mother–initiated dialogues, she responds to Richard's reaction in about 75 per cent of the instances, virtually always giving him full marks for an appropriate communicative intent. A small point adds a sense of the meticulousness of this process. The mother makes a rather sharp distinction between those vocalizations of the child that slot into the dialogue routine of book-reading, and those that are out of place in the exchange. The latter vocalizations and gestures are treated by the mother as procedural—'You like this book, don't you, Richard?' or 'Yes, it's very exciting, isn't it?'—such remarks always addressed to him directly and without reference to the book.

You will be quite right if you infer that the child initially is learning as much about the rules of dialogue as he is about lexical labels. But once the dialogue routine is fully established, at about 18 months or earlier, it becomes the scaffold upon which a new routine is established. For now the mother comes more sharply to distinguish between vocalizations that are 'acceptable' and those that are not. They are now in a 'shaping stage'. Mother tightens the criterion of acceptability as soon as there emerges a sign that the child is trying to produce words. I should warn you that my last sentence includes the whole field of developmental phonology, about which I know just enough to know the depth of my ignorance. But it is not the phonologist's theories that interest us here, but the mother's. When Richard slots in a sound that she thinks too wide of the mark, she will now respond not with a label, but with the question, 'What's that, Richard?' or with a highly emphasized label.

But to put it that way may seem to give too much of a role to pure imitation. Rather, what is notable is that the child does not learn his labels by directly and immediately imitating his mother's labellings. Compare the likelihood of Richard uttering a label during the second half of his second year of life under two conditions. One is in response to the mother's just previously uttered label. The other is in response to his mother's 'What's that?' question. The latter produces four times as many labels as the former. A label for the child is something that slots into a position in a dia-

logue. Indeed, 65 per cent of the labels uttered by Richard
during this second half of the second year were said without
the mother having uttered the label in that exchange. And
an interesting sidelight: Richard responds to 'Wh.. questions'
almost invariably on the first time round. Where he responds
with a label in response to a mother's label, it almost invariably requires at least one repetition by his mother to get him
to do so. We are not, as a species, copy-cats.

One regularity during this shaping phase suggests how crucial is the role of the mother in *teaching* language and its
use. She is constantly establishing linguistic distinctions
between the given and the new, the familiar and unfamiliar.
She is, for example, much more likely to use 'What' questions
with special intonation for pictures the child already knows
and can label easily. New or less familiar pictures are labelled
forthwith. The result is a presuppositional structure about
what one asks about and what one tells.

Perhaps a good way to put the mother's pedagogical role
in perspective is to look at it as providing a stabilizing scaffold during the two phases of label learning we have been
exploring, a stabilizing scaffold with respect to which the
child can vary his responses as his mastery permits. And so
we find, for example, that the time devoted to dialogue
exchange remains constant over these months. The number
of turns in an exchange remains roughly the same. The repetition rate for labelling remains the same. The probability
of the mother's reciprocating the child's response remains
unchanged. And once the child is in the shaping stage, the
mother's rate of confirming correct utterances remains about
the same. All of these are controlled by the mother. They are
what the child can count on in dialogue with her.

What things change over time, on the other hand, are
almost all under the child's control. For one, there is a steady
increase in the number of 'book reading' exchanges initiated
by the child—from 0 per cent to 40 per cent. There is a
steady increase in the child's rate of responding to gestural
or verbal overtures initiated by the mother. He even learns
to respond to repeated, rhetorical requests, ones he has just
answered, suggesting that he is even learning to conform to
the arbitrariness of pedagogical exchanges!

So much then for indexing and referencing. It is a very incomplete story as I have told it, but at least it gives a sense of how related acquisition is to use, to the functions of dialogue and exchange. We turn now to communication in support of joint action.

3. JOINT ACTION AND GRAMMAR

I want very briefly to consider three issues. The first has to do with the precursors of mood in grammar. The second follows from this, as you will see, and concerns the differentiation of joint action into its parts, a matter I have already touched on briefly. And the third has to do with starting, regulating, and stopping joint action.

With respect to mood, let me underline one point made by Catherine Snow. She says: 'One of the most ubiquitous features of . . . mothers' speech at even the earliest age . . . [is that] they constantly talked about the child's wishes, needs, and intentions . . . as if the mother's task was to find out something that the baby already knew . . . Persistent crying was referred to . . . as if it reflected a very well-defined sense of agency; the babies' behaviour was never described as random and only rarely as a function of physiological variables. It was seen, just as adult behaviour was seen, as intended and intentional.' And, indeed, we know from the work of Ricks (1972) that mothers *can* recognize better than chance what general state produces their baby's cry and act accordingly. Not surprising then that the opening months of an infant's life reveal a transformation in the infant's crying from what may be called a demand mode—the standard biological cry, upped when untended to a very wide sound spectrum with a heavy load of high frequency, fricative noise— to a request mode in which energy is concentrated in a fundamental frequency, with the cry stopped for moments at a time in anticipation of response. Request crying gradually achieves stylization and differentiates to match the context— hunger fretting, wet fretting, and so on. By responding to these cries, as already noted, the mother recruits the child's vocalizations from demand and request into more subtle communicative patterns later in the opening year of life (Ainsworth and Bell, 1974). In mood, then, initial crying is transformed from an exigent demand into anticipatory request, with the infant leaving slots for the mother's response.

What follows is the beginning of exchange and turn-taking, first in vocalization and, then, with the growth of manipulative skill, in the exchange of objects—forerunners of dialogue. Danial Stern (1975) has shown exquisitely how mother-infant gesturing and vocalizing become synchronized in the opening months, and our own data on the first half year also show coordinated cycles of eye-contact and calling, controlled principally by the mother, of course, but increasingly by the infant. As the months go on he increasingly initiates acts of vocal exchange. The exchanges then are imbedded in anticipatory body games like 'Round and Round the Garden' and 'This Little Pig', in which vocal exchanges are made contingent on the progress of an interaction and various highbrow technicalities like terminal marking are being mastered in earthy but useful ways.

The next step in interaction appears to be closer to the exchange of objects than to vocalization. Alison Garton, Eileen Caudill and I were led by this to some rather detailed studies of these exchanges, on the hunch that they might serve as a base for later dialogue. You may be amused by a few details of our expedition into the primitive economics of mother–infant exchange. If a market or economy reliable enough to sustain a steady flow of goods is established, can messages then develop that will flow in the same channels? Obviously, the first step for the mother is to get the infant to enter the game of taking objects, which need not concern us though it is of considerable interest as a chapter in the child's increasing capacity to mobilize not only a motoric response but also his attention upon the task (see Bruner, 1973). We have recorded sessions where more than 50 per cent of the time went into the perfecting of this skill. The mother characteristically assumes that the child *wants* the object; what he must be helped to do is *try*. The next step is getting the child to give the object back. If we define agency as handing off, and recipiency as receiving, the child's entry into the exchange economy is steady and striking and surprising to nobody (Fig. 1). Concurrently, another unsurprising but important transition is taking place. Now the child rather than

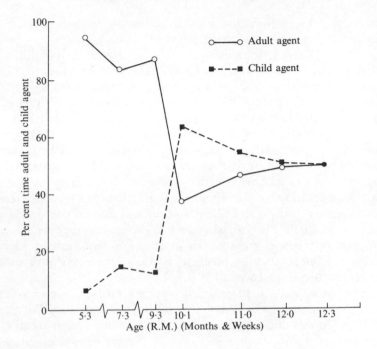

Fig. 1. Shift in role of agent in 'give- and take'. The changing percentages of time the mother and child act as Agent in their interchanges.

the mother alone begins *initiating* exchange episodes (Fig. 2). As he gets into exchange, he is less reluctant to give up an object: his possession time before handing off drops steadily (Fig. 3). Indeed, by 13 months, the concept of exchange itself, rather than the joy of possession, seems to dominate his play. He is able now to enter a *round* of exchange involving two other persons and to maintain the direction of the exchange flow (Fig. 4).

A stunning number of linguistic prerequisites is being mastered. Role shifting is one. Another is turn-taking. A third is the coordination of signalling and acting, for typical of these exchanges is that the child not only hands off the object in minimal time, but looks to the recipient's face as he does so. And should his turn be delayed, he will point, reach, vocalize, or label to get matters righted. Put in the metaphor of case grammar he is differentiating in action

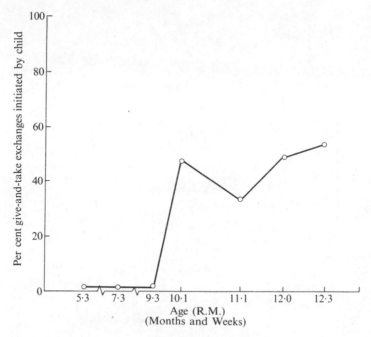

Fig. 2.

between agent and recipient, forming a primitive development of locus with deixis in the sense of knowing to whom the object is to be handed in multiple exchange, learning some elements of time marking in the sense of knowing who comes before and who after. And in addition to all this, the child has come not only to participate in exchanges initiated by others, but to initiate them himself.

I wish there were time and that we had the necessary data fully to describe the manner in which the child during this period learns not only how to start but how to stop the action. For it reveals much about the precursory development of negation as a linguistic form. Initially, negation amounts to no more than a resistive gesture directed toward an act directed to the child; the gesture becomes stylized and is used communicatively. In time, such proto-negation is extended to rejection of a specific object, or a specific agent carrying out an action with an object, or to a temporal mis-

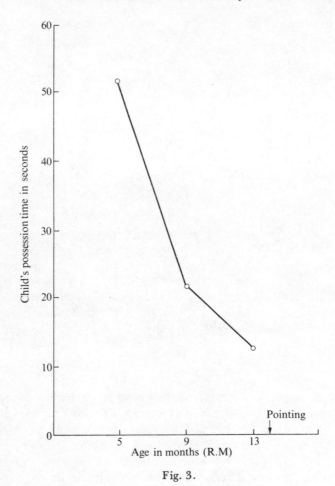

Fig. 3.

placement (as in peekaboo)—all of these directed toward activity initiated by others. Eventually, by 15 months or thereabouts, the child comes to be able to apply negation to his own acts and will approach a forbidden object saying 'No, no' and/or shaking his head. The uses of negation suggest the features of the interaction that the child has singled out conceptually.

I cannot resist mentioning an interesting extension of negation that occurs after the developments just noted, around 17 months, for it suggests yet another instance of the way in

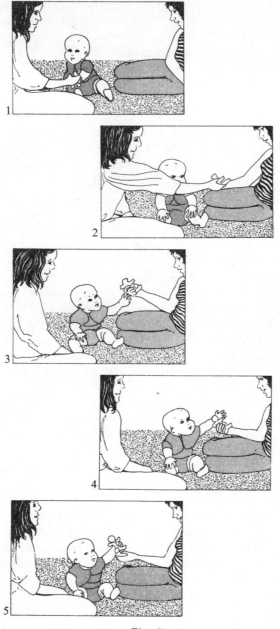

Fig. 4.

which a communicative form is extended to new functions. The new functions in question are more referential than pragmatic. A transitional phase is the use of negation for some mix of unexpectedness and inappropriateness, as when Richard fails tobe able to put a large object into a thin box and utters a well formed 'No'. In his record at that time, there are also instances in which the unexpected absence of an object from a container within which it was expected to be provokes a 'No'. And in the work of Bloom (1973), Greenfield and Smith (1976) and other investigators one finds instances of negation being used for disappearance of an object, self-produced as in 'all-gone' or otherwise produced, or for cessation of an event in the environment. And finally, well into the second year, negation is captured by the rules of dialogue where it can be used for dealing with the linguistic representation of an event contained in a question: 'Do you want more milk?' 'No.' There are various studies now in progress here at Oxford, on propositional negation by Roy Pea and on reference to absent or possible objects by Alison Gopnik, that will shed some light on how eventually negation takes its rightful place as an instrument in specifying truth functionality.

I hope it has been clear from this very brief account of the development of early communication as a means of regulating joint action that language does not grow solely from its own roots but is dependent upon interaction and particularly the interaction of intentions held by two consenting parties, one of them initially willing and able to give the other the benefit of the doubt.

4. SOME UNRESOLVED ISSUES

One last word. I have said very little indeed about the mastery of well-formedness, of grammatical speech *per se*. I am deeply cognizant of the truth of the statement that one cannot learn the rules of grammar from learning the concepts involved in managing interaction and managing joint attention. I have been tempted in the past by the hypothesis that there is something in the deployment of attention that leads naturally to the child adopting the rule that in sentences Agent comes before Action, and Action comes before Object, the near universal SVO order, but I think such assumptions about naturalness lull one into intellectual drowsiness. Rather, I would take the view that the child's knowledge of pre-linguistic communication, related as it is to a world of action and interaction, provides him with tell-tale clues for constructing and testing hypotheses about the meaning and structure of the discourse into which he quickly enters. He does, as LAD would have us believe, have a stunning capacity to infer and to generate rules, indeed to over-genralize them. His hypotheses are based in part upon his knowledge of the requirements of action and of interacting with another. His mother, the tutor, gives him every hint she can. And her hints are first-class, for she is not operating in the dark like a Turing machine. She knows from the start what it will take to speak the native language, and treats the child's efforts from the start as if he *were* a native speaker or were soon to be. Her predictions work out in 99·9 per cent of cases! There may indeed be something innate about the child's ability so swiftly to crack the linguistic code. But there is almost certainly something innate about the mother's ability to help him to do so.

REFERENCES

AINSWORTH, MARY D. and BELL, SYLVIA M., 'Mother–infant interaction and the development of competence.' In K. Connolly and J. S. Bruner (eds.), *The Growth of Competence*, London and New York: Academic Press, 1974.

BLOOM, LOIS, *One Word at a Time: The Use of Single Word Utterances Before Syntax.* The Hague: Mouton, 1973.

BROWN, R., *A First Language: The Early Stages.* Cambridge, Mass.: Harvard University Press, 1973.

BRUNER, J. S., 'Organisation of early skilled action.' *Child Development*, **44**, 1-11, 1973.

CHOMSKY, N., 'Explanatory models in linguistics.' In E. Nagel, P. Suppes and A. Tarski (eds.), *Logic, Methodology and the Philosophy of Science.* Stanford University Press, 1962.

COLLIS, G. and SCHAFFER, H. R., 'Synchronisation of visual attention in mother–infant pairs.' *Journal of Child Psychology and Psychiatry*, **16** (4), 315-20, 1975.

GREENFIELD, PATRICIA M. and SMITH, J. H., *The Structure of Communication in Early Language Development.* New York: Academic Press, 1976.

HARRISON, B., *Meaning and Structure.* New York and London: Harper and Row, 1972.

MACFARLANE, A., 'If a smile is so important.' *New Scientist*, No. 895, 164–6, 25 April 1974.

MCNEILL, D., *The Acquisition of Language: The Study of Developmental Psycholinguistics*. New York: Harper and Row, 1970.

RICKS, D. M., 'The beginnings of vocal communication in infants and autistic children.' Unpublished Doctorate of Medicine thesis, University of London, 1972.

SCAIFE, M. and BRUNER, J. S., 'The capacity for joint visual attention in the infant.' *Nature*, 253 (5489), 265–6, 1975.

SHVACHKIN, N. Kh., 'The development of phonemic speech perception in early childhood.' *Izvestiya Akademii Pedagogcheskikh Nauk RSFSR*, 13, 101–32, 1948. Translated from Russian by E. Dernback and edited by D. I. Slobin, in C. A. Ferguson and D. I. Slobin (eds.), *Studies of Child Language Development*. New York: Holt, Rinehart and Winston, 91–127, 1973.

SNOW, CATHERINE E., 'The development of conversation between mothers and babies.' *Journal of Child Language*, in press.

STERN, D., JAFFE, J., BEEBE, B., and BENNETT, S., 'Vocalising in unison and in alternation: two modes of communication within the mother–infant dyad.' Paper presented at the Conference on Developmental Psycholinguistics and Communication Disorder, New York Academy of Sciences, New York, January 1975. (Published in *The Transactions of the New York Academy of Sciences*.)

4 From Gesture to Word: On the Natural History of Deixis in Language Acquisition[1]

EVE V. CLARK

One thing that has become very clear in the study of language acquisition is that children play an active role in the acquisition process itself. They do not just pick up language because they hear it around them. They actively form hypotheses about its meaning and from these derive strategies for using it. Take one child's use of *come* in the utterance 'She came it over there', said as she watched a dog take a piece of food into the next room (Bowerman, 1974). This child had used *come* earlier with the meaning 'move'. She then hypothesized that it could also mean 'cause to move' on the pattern of *walk* in *The dog walked* and *The man walked the dog*, and adopted the strategy of using *come* when she wanted to talk about something either moving or being made to move. Although this is a very specific example, it provides a good illustration of two ideas that pervade much of development—continuity and the use of strategies.

Take continuity. In the illustration just given, the child's use of *come* with the meaning 'cause to move' developed out of her use of *come* with the meaning of 'move'. Many such continuities can be seen in language development. Children basically build on what they already know. For instance, the objects they attend to and pick out with gestures tend to be the same ones that are later named in single word utterances, namely objects that can move (e.g. daddy, kitty, car), and objects that are moveable (e.g. bottle, shoe, block), plus a few places (e.g. chair, box), recipients (e.g. mummy),

[1] The preparation of this paper was supported in part by the National Science Foundation, Grant No. SOC75–17126, and in part by a Mellon Fellowship from Stanford University. I would like to thank Herbert H. Clark for his invaluable suggestions on an earlier version of this paper.

and instruments (e.g. spoon—for eating; block—for making a noise). The relationships picked out by single words—movers or agents of an action, moveable objects, or places, for example—are the same ones later picked out by two word utterances, e.g. *Mummy read*, *Put shoe*, *Baby chair*. The expression of negation provides yet another example: children start with gestures alone—pushing away unwanted food or resisting being dressed—then replace these with single word utterances like. *no* or *not*. Later they make what is being negated more explicit, e.g. *No go out*, *No bed*, and later still produce even more complex expressions like *I don't want to go out*, or *It's not bedtime yet*. Continuities like these allow one to trace the developmental paths children follow as they acquire their first language.

And take strategies. Children seem to come up with hypotheses about what words mean and from these derive strategies for their use. For example, after hearing the word *dog*, a child might come up with the hypothesis that *dog* serves to pick out objects that are mammal-shaped (with a head, body, and four legs). Having set up this hypothesis, the child derives from it strategies for using *dog*. For example, whenever he hears *dog* from others, he will look around until he finds an appropriate object. With this strategy for comprehension, the child should do fairly well since adults will usually be talking to him about the here-and-now. And whenever he himself wants to draw someone else's attention to a mammal-shaped object for which he has no other name, he will say the word *dog*. This strategy for production may not be quite as successful as the comprehension one because the child may use *dog* to pick out horses and cows as well as dogs until he learns additional category names. Eventually, he must adjust his hypothesis about *dog* to the point where his strategies for use coincide with the adult's.

The strategies children derive from their hypotheses throw a good deal of light not only on the form of their initial hypotheses about different meanings but also on the changes that take place in their hypotheses as they learn more about the adult meaning of particular words and utterances. Changes in strategy reflect changes in the hypothesis. And the strategies children use also serve to show whether they all

come up with the same hypothesis about a new word—
whether the hypothesis is right or wrong—or whether some
come up with one hypothesis and some with another. In fact,
children do not necessarily all follow the same route in working out particular adult meanings. For example, where one
child takes *dog* to mean 'mammal-shaped object', another
may take it to mean 'soft and furry object'. This difference
would affect their strategies for use in an obvious way.

In this paper I shall take up these two themes—continuity
and strategy—in presenting a natural history of deixis, of how
children acquire *deictic* or 'pointing' words: pronouns like
I or *you*, locatives and demonstratives like *here* or *that*,
and verbs like *come* or *go*. In the first part, I describe some
of the properties of deictic terms, their dimensions of contrast, their relative complexity, and their relation to definite
reference. In the second part, I take up the origins of deixis
in the pointing gestures used by adult and child. In children,
there is continuity in their progress from deictic gestures to
deictic words. In the third part, I examine some of the hypotheses and strategies that children bring to the acquisition of
the contrasts between deictic pairs like *here* and *there* or
come and *go*.

DEICTIC TERMS IN ENGLISH

Deictic terms, deictics, or indexicals are words that 'pick
out' or 'point to' things in relation to the participants in the
speech situation. In doing so, they anchor each utterance to
the context in which it was produced. Person deixis, for
example, picks out the different participants and people
talked about in a conversation with pronouns like *I, we,
you,* or *they.* Place deixis uses locative or demonstrative
terms like *here* or *that* to pick out places and objects, and
verbs like *come* and *go* to pick out motion towards or away
from some point of reference (Fillmore, 1966, 1971; Clark,
1974). Time deixis uses verb tense and adverbs like *now* and
yesterday to anchor the time referred to in each utterance
to the actual time of speaking (see further Kuryłowicz,
1964; Fillmore, 1971; Traugott, 1975). In this paper I will
limit my discussion to the five major pairs of terms used in
person and place deixis shown in Table 1.

Table 1
Deictic Contrasts in English

1. *I—you*	Speaker
2. *here—there*	Speaker & Place
3. *this—that*	Speaker & Place & Object
4. *come—go*	Speaker & Place & Object & Movement
5. *bring—take*	Speaker & Place & Object & Movement & Cause

Deictic terms anchor each utterance by reference to the speaker in the here and now. This notion of speaker is central to each of the pairs in Table 1. In their simplest uses, for example, the pronoun *I* picks out the speaker in contrast to *you*—the person being addressed. The locative *here* picks out the place where the speaker is in contrast to *there*—a place where the speaker is not. *This* and *that* are like *here* and *there* but the contrast is more complicated because the terms pick out an object that is either at the place where the speaker is (*this*) or not (*that*). Finally, in their basic uses, the verbs *come, go, bring* and *take* pick out the movement of a person or object towards (*come, bring*) or away from (*go, take*) the place where the speaker is, or was, or expects to be (see further Fillmore, 1971). Note that *bring* and *take* mean roughly 'cause to come' and 'cause to go', respectively.

This simple analysis of these pairs shows that the notion common to them all is that of *speaker*. It plays a major role in the contrast between *I* and *you*, and combines with notions like *place, object, movement* and *cause* in the other deictic pairs in Table 1. The right-hand side of Table 1, therefore, provides a rough measure of the inherent complexity of different deictic contrasts. The first, between *I* and *you*, appears to be the simplest, with the others becoming progressively more complex as more notions are involved in their meanings. Of course, these notions do not in any way constitute a formal semantic analysis of these deictic terms. Nor do they include all the components that may be necessary in such an analysis. At the same time, they do represent the general concepts that children have to group together in order to learn how to use each pair of deictic terms. *A priori,* then, it seems reasonable to expect that these deictic contrasts will be acquired in the order listed.

Two factors make deictic terms rather complicated from the child's point of view: *shifting reference* and *shifting boundaries*.

1. *Shifting reference.* Deictic terms all involve shifting reference. For example, whoever is the speaker at the moment is the person allowed to use *I* in self-reference. And that person uses *you* to his addressee. But the referents of *I* and *you* can change with every change of speaker in a conversation. Compare this shifting reference with the invariable reference of proper names and category names: the name *Katherine* and the noun *table* do not change their reference in a particular context when there is a change of speaker. Having agreed to call someone Katherine or some object a table, each speaker uses the same terms. The problem of shifting reference is also inherent in the use of *here* and *there*, *this* and *that*, *come* and *go*, and *bring* and *take*.

Shifting reference makes deictic terms an exception, as far as children are concerned, because they constitute a case where the 'name' *doesn't* go with the object designated. Children have to work out that shifting reference always turns on who the speaker is. The shift of speaker to *I* is constant with each change of speaker, but *you* can be used to pick out different addressees in the course of a single conversational turn with a single speaker. *You*, in other words, may involve even more shifting reference than *I*. This suggests that of the two pronouns, *I* may be easier to acquire. Other pronouns like *he, she*, and *they* can shift even more frequently than *you* in conversation and so should be even more difficult to master. If shifting reference is a major determinant of order of acquisition, *I* should be acquired first, followed by *you* second, and *he, she, it*, and *they* third. Similar considerations probably affect the acquisition of other deictic terms as well.

2. *Shifting boundaries. Here, there, this,* and *that* are used with shifting boundaries. *Here* can be used to pick out the precise spot on the floor where the speaker is standing (*here where I am*), the room he is in (*here in the study*), the town (*here in Oxford*), the country (*here in Britain*),

and so on. *There*, in each instance simply picks out a place beyond the implicit or explicit boundary of 'here'. The same is true of *this* and *that*.

Becuase of the shifting boundary, anything could be included within the space picked out by *here*, but there is a restriction on what can be included in *there*. It cannot include the place where the speaker is. The same restriction applies to the demonstrative *that*. This suggests that the notion of being near the speaker is a primary one. As a result, it may be easier for children to grasp the notion 'near the speaker' than 'relatively far from the speaker' in the acquisition of the contrast between *here* and *there*, and *this* and *that*.

Shifting boundaries, combined with shifting reference, should make it hard to work out how deictic terms are applied and also how precisely they contrast with each other.

The use of deictic terms is closely linked to definite reference. Terms like *here* or *that* pick out specific objects for the listener in the same way that the definite article *the* does. Where a small child says *That mine* or *Book here*, an adult may say *The chair is mine* or *The book is on the table*. In fact, some linguists have argued that the definite article *the* is itself derived from a deictic locative phrase of roughly the form 'which is there'. The noun phrase *the man*, for example, would have an underlying structure that could be represented as 'man who is there' (Thorne, 1972, 1974). This suggests that children's notions of definite reference are built on their earlier use of deictic expressions like *here* or *that* to pick out or point to specific objects for their listeners (Antinucci, 1974; Lyons, 1975). Deictic reference, then, is definite reference and should meet all the requirements placed on definite reference.[2]

---

[2] Several investigators have focused specifically on children's acquisition of the definite and indefinite articles to convey what is given and what is new information to the listener. *The* tags things as given, judged by the speaker to be identifiable by the listener; *a* tags things as new, judged by the speaker as not already known to the listener. Their general findings are the following: Children begin to use both the definite and the indefinite article with nouns from 2;6 or so onwards, but they tend to use the definite much more frequently than the indefinite (Carroll, 1939). By taking into account the context of use, investigators have found that the younger the children, the more they over-estimate what their listeners know: they over-use the definite article in places where adults use the indefinite one to present new information (see Maratsos, 1976; Warden, 1976;

What are the requirements for definite reference? First, there are cognitive prerequisites for being able to pick out an object or event for someone else, for a 'listener'. In general, this demands that the speaker (and the listener) know three things about objects: that they have an independent existence, apart from the speaker and listener; that they can be individuated; and that they belong to classes. These distinctions are ones that infants begin to learn very early, during their first year of life.

1. *Existence*. From the moment infants begin to look around, to touch, grasp, and mouth the different objects within their reach, they begin to work on the existence of other objects. Realizing that they exist independently of the person picking them out, even if they are not in sight, is essential for making reference. A strong test of this realization on the infant's part is Piaget's (1954) device of taking an object and hiding it under a blanket in full view of an infant. According to Piaget, only those infants who have a notion of object permanence will later look for the object in the place where it was hidden. But for infants who still lack part of this notion, the object 'ceases to exist' once it is out of sight. By the age of one, many (perhaps most) children pass this 'test' of Piaget's and thus show their awareness that objects have an independent existence.

2. *Individuation*. As children come to realize that objects have an independent existence, they also begin to pick out individual objects such as their own blankets, the family pet, their own bowls or mugs, and so on. For example, infants begin to recognize faces from about eight months on. And unexpected changes in an object are readily noticed by quite young infants. If they are watching a ball move behind a screen and it reappears at the other side in the form of a cube, they are demonstrably surprised (see Bower, 1974).

3. *Class-membership*. In learning how to pick out specific objects during their first year, infants also learn which objects are alike in certain respects and which are different. They

---

Bresson, 1974). The contrasting uses of the definite for given and the indefinite for new information does not seem to be mastered until the age of eight or so. It may therefore depend on prior mastery of the deictic terms *here*, *there*, *this*, and *that* (see below).

find out, for example, that you drink from bottles or mugs, sit on chairs, sleep in beds, and so on. Bottles and chairs, then, belong to different classes—they look different and they are treated differently. But two chairs will be treated alike—they look similar and their function is the same, they are both for sitting on. Children build up their knowledge of class-membership from the general knowledge they acquire about the world around them, and by the age of one they know a good deal about individual objects and their class-membership.

These cognitive prerequisites for reference are all met before children begin to speak, usually between the age of one and two years. These prerequisites turn out to be very similar to those postulated by John Searle (1969) in his discussion of the speech act of definite reference. He argued that two axioms have to be satisfied in order for one to make a definite reference. By the *axiom of existence*, the objects talked about have to have an independent existence. This axiom coincides with the first cognitive prerequisite. By the *axiom of identity*, the speaker has to be able to identify for his listener any object that he talks about: 'If a speaker refers to an object, then he identifies or is able on demand to identify that object for the hearer apart from all other objects' (p. 79). This axiom appears to correspond to the second and third cognitive prerequisites—the individuation of objects and their class-membership.

The listener may not always be able to identify the object from the speaker's act of definite reference. In the limit, therefore, the speaker may satisfy the axiom of identity by *showing* the listener the object he is referring to. For adults, this is a last resource. But for children, this limiting case is actually their starting-point for making definite reference. At first, they can only *show* their 'listeners' what they are referring to. Later on, they learn how to *tell* them. The natural history of deixis, therefore, starts when children begin to show things to their 'listeners'.

THE ORIGINS OF DEIXIS

Children pick out objects for others first with gestures alone and later with gestures and words combined. In this

section, I take up the evidence for this argument in considering how children go from gestural deixis—pointing and showing—to linguistic deixis—using words to pick out objects.
I first describe when infants begin to use gestures and the
extent to which they seem to make them with a 'listener'
in mind. Then I shall look at the first deictic words in children's speech and their use in conjunction with earlier deictic
gestures. Thirdly, I shall consider some inherent limitations
on the use of gestures to accompany deictic words and suggest that these limitations may explain why most languages
have evolved systems of deictic contrast that encode relative
proximity to the speaker.

Gestures and 'listeners'

Small infants begin to respond to adult gestures and
attempts to gain their attention very early. And they soon
reciprocate by showing things to adults in return. Escalona
(1973) documented the following sequence of development
in the emergence of reciprocal behaviour between adult
and child. Once infants reach the age of three months or so,
adults begin to offer them things—a toy, a corner of blanket,
a finger—and show them things—holding up a bell, a mirror,
or a toy in the infant's field of vision and moving it or
making a noise to attract attention. By the time infants are
six months old, they begin to reciprocate by showing and
offering things in return, holding up a toy or a ball and dis-
playing it near the adult's face. At this stage, adults expand
their range of operations: they begin to point to things that
are further away from the infant and they attempt to direct
his gaze to different objects in the room. They have moved,
as it were, from the immediate vicinity of the child's cot or
playpen to the wider confines of the room or the garden.
The pointing and gazing introduced by adults begin to appear
in the infant's repertoire at about nine or ten months of age.

The emergent reciprocity, with both adults and infants
holding objects out to the other or pointing, is not necessarily being done for the 'listener'—the other. The issue here
is whether infant gestures like this are merely learned responses or whether they have a real communicative function.
If infant pointing, for example, were simply a learned response, one might expect to find it limited to objects that the

infant had observed the adult pointing at, and the infant's use of pointing should not be dependent on whether there is a 'listener' there or not. While this has yet to be investigated, other studies strongly suggest that by the age of one pointing does have a communicative function for the infant. He not only uses pointing to show to another what he is interested in, but he also responds to pointing in others by looking at the object indicated.

Bates (1976), for example, found the following sequence of development after the emergence of pointing in the Italian children she studied:

(1) The children would point and stare at whatever caught their attention from the age of ten months on.

(2) Within a few weeks, they began to check whether their 'listener' was attending or not in the following way: they would point and look, then swing both hands and gaze round to point at the adult and see whether he was attending, and then they would swing their hand and gaze back again to point to the object of interest.

(3) Finally, by the age of one, the children could stare and point, turn their heads to look at the adult without moving their hand, and then turn their gaze back to whatever had attracted their attention to begin with.

From the second stage on, they would make deliberate efforts to attract the adult's attention if he wasn't looking when they monitored. They would make a noise or whine, or even go over to the adult and touch his hand or clothing in order to get his attention. This checking up on the 'listener' shows that pointing for children of this age already has a communicative function, for in order to communicate anything, the 'speaker' must first make sure that the 'listener' is attending (see also Bates, Camaioni, and Volterra, 1975; Bates, Benigni, Bretherton, Camaioni, and Volterra, 1976; Bruner, 1975; Werner and Kaplan, 1963).

Other investigators have studied not only the spontaneous use or production of pointing for others, but also its comprehension by children of this age. Lempers, Flavell, and Flavell (1977) found that most children aged one and one and a half spontaneously point at objects that catch their attention (see also Rheingold, 1973). To find out whether the same children understood pointing done by others, they took each child into a small room where there was an adult already in position pointing at something. The adults imply called the child's name to get his attention and then observers noted where the child looked—at the adult's face, at his hand, or in the direction the hand was pointing. (In this situation, the children saw no hand motion as the adult was already pointing when they first saw him.) All the one-and-a-half-year-olds looked in the direction pointed, as did over half the one-year-olds. The remaining children looked either at the adult's hand or at his face. These findings demonstrate very clearly that by one to one and a half, children understand the function of pointing—to direct one's attention—even when they have not seen any movement associated with an action of pointing. Their comprehension as well as their production of pointing is communicative in nature.

Deictic words and gestures

Children continue to point and gesture after they begin to use their first words. Words are probably more effective in some contexts in getting the listener's attention since children no longer have to rely on getting the 'listener' to look at them first. Among the earliest words acquired is usually at least one deictic word—a word invariably used together with a deictic gesture. A deictic word based on *there* or *that*, with the form [e], [a?], or [da], often appears in the first ten words of English-speaking children, certainly within the first 50 or so (e.g. Nelson, 1973; Nice, 1915; Grant, 1915). And diarists describing the acquisition of languages as diverse as Bulgarian, Dutch, German, and Japanese report much the same thing (e.g. Gheorgov, 1905; van der Geest, 1974; Lindner, 1898; Sanches, 1968). These early deictic words are always accompanied by pointing and intent staring at the object of interest (see Leopold, 1949; Werner and Kaplan, 1963; De Laguna, 1927). They also tend to be among the most frequently used of the child's early words (e.g. Bloom, 1970; Weir, 1962).

Pointing continues to accompany deictic words like *here* or *that* when children move from single words to longer utterances. Bloom (1970), for example, noted that one of the children she studied, Kathryn, *invariably* pointed whenever she used a two-word utterance containing deictic *that*, e.g. *That chair* (see also Rodgon, 1976). Snyder (1914) noted a similar use of gesture with *that* (in the form *dat*), especially when her child was picking out two objects. He would indicate first one and then the other with gestures. It is only considerably later, after children have learned to contrast *this* with *that* or *here* with *there*, that they will give up using gestures in some contexts.[3]

The stages children seem to go through as they move from gestures to words in making deictic reference can be roughly summarized as in Table 2. At the first stage, children use gestures like pointing to pick out an object for their 'listeners'. At the second, they add to their gesture their first deictic word, often of the form *eh* (from adult *there*) or *da* (from adult *that*). Later still, at a third stage, they combine a deictic word with other words to form longer utterances like *That shoe*, or *That mine*, and accompany their utterances with a gesture. Finally, at a fourth stage, they learn how to use deictic words in utterances without any accompanying gesture. The third and fourth stages are probably widely separated in time. And the final stage is really one in which gestures become optional. Adults, for instance, gesture continually for children to get them to attend (Garnica, 1975; Collis, 1977; Murphy and Messer, 1977; Shatz, 1974). In many settings, though, adults dispense with gestures and rely on deictic words alone.

Limitations on deictic gestures

Although deictic gestures are used extensively by both adults and children, there are certain limitations on how informative they can be. A pointing gesture identifies a vector in which the 'listener/observer' is expected to search. But suppose there are two objects, a chair and a box, one beyond the other, in the vector indicated. Pointing alone cannot tell

---

[3] Adults use gesture and gaze in conjunction with deictic words and may find it very hard to refrain from using them, especially with *here, there, this,* and *that.*

Table 2
From Deictic Gesture to Deictic Word

Stage	Gesture		Utterance
1	point		
2	point	+	*da* (= that)
3	point	+	*that shoe*
4			*that coat is mine*

the observer which of the two the 'speaker' is trying to pick out. This obstacle can be overcome, of course, as soon as a child learns to name objects. He can combine his gesture with the word for the one he is picking out, e.g. 'Point + *box*'. But a more complicated obstacle still lies ahead. Suppose there are two *identical* objects, two chairs, one beyond the other, in the vector indicated. Naming is of no help in this situation because the word *chair* does not discriminate between the two chairs. Something more than a gesture-word combination is needed in this case.

The option that has been taken in most languages is to distinguish deictically between two objects by indicating their relative distance from a reference point, the speaker himself. This choice of reference point is eminently reasonable since it is the speaker who is trying to convey to the listener which of the two objects he is interested in. If the speaker has a way of using relative distance along the line of sight to pick out objects, he can always make clear to his listener which one he is concerned with, the one nearer him or the one further away.

Deictic distinctions based on relative distance are very common. In English, the terms *here* and *this* pick out objects that are relatively near the speaker (proximal) while *there* and *that* pick out objects that are further away (non-proximal). In French, the locative particles *-ci* and *-là*, combined with the demonstrative *ce* play the same role. The expression *ce livre-ci* picks out a book relatively close to the speaker, *ce livre-là* a book that is further away. The same type of contrast appears in many other languages too (Frei, 1944; Kurłowicz, 1964). A few languages, like Spanish, even have a three-way deictic contrast: 'here' near the speaker, 'there' further away from the speaker but in sight, and 'over there' further away still, on the horizon or out of sight. English itself used to contrast *here*, *there*, and *yon* in much the same way.

Young children, however, do not use their first deictic words contrastively. *There*, for example, serves to pick out objects near the speaker as well as ones that are further away. The accompanying gesture at this stage tells the listener which object the speaker is concerned with. In the acquisition of deixis, therefore, children have not only to learn which terms are deictic but also how different deictic terms contrast with each other. They have to learn, for example, that *here* and *there* contrast in meaning along the proximal–nonproximal dimension, while *come* and *go* contrast in whether the motion is towards or away from the speaker. The acquisition of these contrasts takes a long time.

STRATEGIES IN THE ACQUISITION OF DEICTIC CONTRASTS

In the course of working out the contrast between deictic terms like *I* and *you*, or *here* and *there*, children apply different strategies, the outcomes of their changing hypotheses. The acquisition of such contrasts can be roughly characterized by three stages: first no contrast, followed by an incorrect or partial contrast, followed by the full adult contrast.

1. *No contrast*. At this stage, children usually use only one of a deictic pair. For example, they may use *here*, combined with pointing, to indicate objects that are far away as well as ones close by.

2. *Partial contrast*. As soon as children add another deictic word—*there*, for instance—to the *here* already in use, they have to work out how the terms are related in meaning, how they contrast. Their initial hypotheses are often either incorrect or incomplete. They may focus on a particular context for *there* and base their hypothesis on its use in expressions like *There you are*, said as the adult hands the child a mended toy or an opened box. Under these circumstances, a child might decide that *there* indicates something being transferred to him or the completion of some action—both hypotheses that miss the deictic meaning of *there*. Or child-

ren may work out only part of the deictic contrast to begin with. For example, they might realize that distance with respect to some reference point was involved with expressions like *in here* and *out there*, but not realize that the reference point is always the speaker.

3. *Full (adult) contrast.* By this stage, children have adjusted their initial hypotheses about the nature of the contrast between *here* and *there* and worked out that it is based on relative proximity to the speaker.

These three stages capture the path children seem to follow in working out successive deictic contrasts. The first to be acquired is that between the pronouns *I* and *you*. The second is the contrast between the locatives *here* and *there*, followed shortly by the one between the demonstratives *this* and *that*. Last of all, they work out the contrasts between the verbs *come* and *go*, and *bring* and *take*. In other words, children work out the least complex contrast before they advance to more complex ones (see Table 1). The first deictic contrast, between *I* and *you*, appears at about 2;6 or 3;0, and the last appears several years later, at around age 8;0.

I and *you*

The first pronoun children use is a 'first person' form such as *I, me, my,* or *mine* (e.g. Foulke and Stinchfield, 1929; Bain, 1936; Leopold, 1949; Ames, 1952; Huxley, 1970). It is used only sporadically to begin with, usually in alternation with the child's own name or *baby* used in self-reference. For example, children may use *I do it* alongside *Ali do it, My book* alongside *Baby book*, or *I jump* alongside *Timmy jump*.

As long as children are using only some form of *I*, they seem to be quite unconcerned by its shifting reference—the fact that other people also use *I*. The children's first use of *I* for self-reference always seems to be correct. However, it is possible that some of its earliest uses are simply formulaic. It is part of a set phrase or formula such as *I can do it!* or *Me too!* and has no independent status until the children manage to analyse these utterances and segment out the pronoun forms.

The next pronoun children use is *you*. Once they have added it, they have to decide on its relation to *I*. *A priori*, there are two plausible hypotheses they could entertain. One is that pronouns are a type of name. Children might notice that the *you* used in addressing them is an alternative to their names. And the *I* used by the adult speaker is an alternative name too, an alternative, for example, to Mummy or Daddy. They therefore focus on the use of *you* in reference to themselves and *I* in reference to adults or people other than themselves:

> *Hypothesis 1*   I   = adult
>   you = child

This hypothesis conforms to the general rule of non-shifting reference.

The second hypothesis is that pronouns like *I* and *you* have a shifting reference that follows the speaker and addressee: they observe that when the speaker says *I am eating*, he is the one carrying out the action. And when he says *You're putting your boots on*, the *you* picks out the person doing the action, this time someone other than the speaker. By paying attention to whoever is carrying out an action or being described in some way, children can seize on the shifting reference of *I* and *you* from the start and link it to the speaker:

> *Hypothesis 2*   I   = speaker
>   you = addressee

It is possible, of course, that children who start off with Hypothesis 2 work out the contrast between *I* and *you* before beginning to use *you*. They therefore seem to get it right from the very start.

Most children in fact seem to begin with the second hypothesis and have little difficulty in contrasting *I* and *you* with each other or with other pronouns acquired later on. The remainder seem to start with the first hypothesis—that *you* is used to refer to themselves (to children) and *I* to adults. The result is that they may spend as much as six months (roughly from 2;0 to 2;6 or so) using *I* and *you* for adults and children, respectively, rather than for speaker and addressee. Later, this hypothesis is abandoned in favour of shifting reference, and by age 2;6 or 3;0, most children have worked out the precise adult contrast between *I*—the speaker—and *you*—the addressee.

But what happens when children start out with this wrong hypothesis? Typically, they use *you* in self-reference as in the following dialogue between Nigel, aged 1;11, on his way to bed, and his mother (Halliday, 1975):

Mother	What do you want?	
Nigel	Daddy toothbrush	
Mother	Oh you want Daddy's toothbrush, do you?	
Nigel	Yes . . . you want to put the frog in the mug.	(you = I)
Mother	I think the frog is too big for the mug.	
Nigel	Yes you can put the duck in the mug . . .	
	make bubble . . . make bubble.	(you = I)
Mother	Tomorrow. Nearly all the water's run out.	
Nigel	You want Mummy red toothbrush . . . yes	
	you can have Mummy old red toothbrush.	(you = I)

For Nigel, *I* was reserved for addressing adults.

Other investigators have made similar observations. Cooley (1908) found that his third child used *I* for adults and *you* for children for about four months after the introduction of *you* into her speech (i.e. from age 1;11 to 2;3). The following utterances were typical of her usage at this stage:

I carry you	(= you carry me)
You'll fall	(said of self when falls down)
I carry	(= you carry; a request to be picked up)
Yacky tease you	(= Yacky is teasing me)
I take you	(= you take me)
Papa help you	(= Papa help me)
You want cake	(= I want cake)
I don't want to bite you	(= you don't want to bite me)

Jespersen (1922) noted similar uses of *I* and *you* in Danish children. One, Frans, consistently used *you* for himself and *I* for adults from the age of 2;0 to 2;6, e.g.

Will I tell a story?	(= will you tell a story?)

The same hypothesis was observed by van der Geest (1975) in his own child, aged 2;2, acquiring Dutch, and by Savić (1974) in twins acquiring Serbian, e.g.

Dutch

Jij doet dat.	('You do that' = I do that)
Ik moet dat maken; dat kan jij niet.	('I must mend that; you can't' = You must mend that; I can't)

Serbian

Ti oće jos̀.	('You want more' = I want more)
Ti tiku.	('You uncle' [request to see her uncle] = I uncle)

Further examples are reported by Sully (1896), Shipley and Shipley (1969), and Sharpless (1974).

The use of *I* for adults and *you* for children usually extends to the possessive pronouns *my* and *your* too, as observations by Cooley, Jespersen, and van der Geest illustrate:

Mama go get my lapboard.	(my = your)
Take my leg up.	(my = your [request to adult to move leg])
That's YOUR chair; that's YOUR chair!	(your = my [child jealous of older sister touching her things making an emphatic claim of possession])
Is dit jouw melk?	('Is this your milk?' = is that my milk)

Notice that all the utterances cited so far sound perfectly normal. It is only in context that it is possible to detect such mis-use of *I* and *you*.

The wrong hypothesis about *I* and *you* may take several months to correct. The misunderstandings that result both in them and in adults may well play some role in causing such children to change their hypothesis. By the time these children have arrived at the right hypothesis, they will have gone through the three general stages mentioned earlier. They first used the pronoun *I* alone, with no contrast; then they used *I* and *you* with a wrong contrast; and finally came to use *I* and *you* appropriately, with the contrast adults use.

Here and *there* and *this* and *that*

There or *that* generally provides the model for the first deictic term children pick up, and it is always accompanied by some kind of pointing gesture. By 2;6 or 3;0, many children have begun to use both *here* and *there*, or *this* and *that*, in their spontaneous speech. Do they contrast the members of each pair in any way? Huxley (1970) reported that she could find no evidence of any proximal/non-proximal contrast between *this* and *that* in two children she followed from the age of 2;3 up to 4;0. This suggests that any contrast children might have between terms like *here* and *there* is unrelated to their deictic meaning. Griffiths (1974) reported just such a case: a child who reserved *here* for deictic reference (with accompanying gestures) and *there* for marking the completion of an action with the meaning 'finished' or 'done'.

Word collocations—common combinations of certain words—provide another potential source of initial contrast between such pairs. For example, *here* may occur very frequently in expressions like *Come here, Give it here,* and *In here!,* while *there* occurs in *There you are, There you go,* and *Over there!* Expressions like these may appear as well-worn formulae in children's speech and make it appear that they have a deictic contrast between *here* and *there* before they really do.

Although children probably make mistakes in the use of *here* and *there,* and *this* and *that,* much as they do earlier with *I* and *you,* these mistakes are very hard to detect. The reason for this lies in the shifting boundary that goes with such pairs. As I pointed out earlier, *here* can pick out the precise spot where the speaker is standing, or the room she is in, or the town, or the country, and so on. *There* then picks out a place beyond the implicit or explicit boundary set for *here.* When children use *here* and *there,* the boundary is virtually always implicit so mistakes are very hard to catch. A few observers, though, have noticed the occasional error. Van der Geest (1975) reported that his son Mark, having mastered the contrast between *I* and *you,* went through a phase of using *there* for his own location, as in the following dialogue at age 2;6:

Father	Mark waar ben je? ('Mark, where are you?')
Mark	(out of sight) Ik ben daar; in de slaapkamer. ('I am there; in the bedroom')

In Dutch as in English, the use of *here* with *I* is mandatory in this context.

Since children make so few detectable errors in production, C. J. Sengul and I decided to study their comprehension in order to find out when they acquired the contrast between *here* and *there* and *this* and *that*, and what hypotheses and strategies they entertained in working out these contrasts (Clark and Sengul, 1974, 1977). We tested their comprehension in the situation shown schematically in Fig. 1. Each child was seated at a low table with the speaker sitting beside him in one condition (Speaker$_1$) and opposite in the other (Speaker$_2$). In front of the child were two equidistant discs of coloured cardboard, placed on the arc of his arm's length reach with one circle near the edge of the table where he was seated (the near circle) and one near the other side of the table (the far circle). Two identical toy animals were placed on the table, one in each circle; and the speaker then gave each child instructions like 'Make the horse over here/there jump up and down' or 'Make this/that horse turn round', and noted which of the two animals the child manipulated.

The age-range studied went from 2;7—an age at which many children have begun to use both *here* and *there*—up to 5;3, about a year beyond the age for which Huxley (1970) reported no discernible contrast between *this* and *that*. Each child received instructions containing *here, there, this,* and

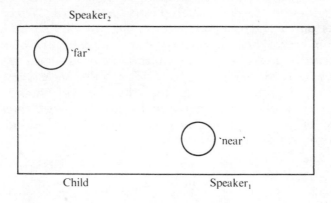

Fig. 1. Testing Deictic Contrasts: *Here* and *There*. (From Clark and Sengul, 1974.) Table used in comprehension experiments, showing the positions of the circles ('near' and 'far') in which the objects were placed, of the two speakers and of the seated child.

that, both with the speaker sitting beside them and with the speaker opposite.

In acquiring these terms, children went through three distinct stages. The youngest ones made no contrast between *here* and *there* or *this* and *that* in responding to the instructions. At an intermediate stage, the children did contrast *here* with *there* and *this* with *that* part of the time, but the rest of the time they made no contrast. Finally, among the oldest children, a number made a full contrast between the deictic terms, taking *here* and *this* to indicate proximity to the speaker and *there* and *that* relative distance away from the speaker.

Close scrutiny of the patterns of errors showed that children followed different paths through the no contrast and partial contrast stages. At the no contrast stage, the error-patterns revealed two distinct groups. Some children appeared to have started with a *child-centred* hypothesis about the meanings of *here* and *there*—that the object picked out was near to the child. They therefore relied on the strategy of choosing the toy in the near circle (Fig. 1) whatever the instruction. As a result, they happened to get *here* 'right' and *there* 'wrong' when the speaker was sitting next to them. They also selected the toy in the near circle when the speaker was sitting opposite, but because of the speaker's position, they got *here* 'wrong' and *there* 'right'. The outcome of the child-centred strategy is shown in Table 3.

Table 3
Child–centred Strategy with No Contrast

	Speaker beside		Speaker opposite	
Instruction:	here	there	here	there
Choice:	near circle (right)	near circle (wrong)	near circle (wrong)	near circle (right)

Based on Clark and Sengul (1974)

Other children appeared to start with a *speaker-centred* hypothesis, that the deictic words in the instructions picked out objects near the speaker. When the speaker was sitting beside them, they did exactly what the child-centred children did: they always manipulated the toy in the near circle, regardless of the instruction. And they too got *here* 'right' and *there* 'wrong'. However, when the speaker was sitting opposite, these children chose the toy in the far circle instead, again regardless of the instruction. The far circle, of course, was the one closest to the speaker in the opposite condition. The children therefore got *here* 'right' again and *there* 'wrong'. The outcome of the speaker-centred strategy is shown in Table 4.

Table 4
Speaker–centred Strategy with No Contrast

	Speaker beside		Speaker opposite	
Instruction:	here	there	here	there
Choice:	near circle (right)	near circle (wrong)	far circle (right)	far circle (wrong)

Based on Clark and Sengul (1974)

At the intermediate stage, all the children made a partial contrast between *here* and *there*. They made the contrast correctly either when the speaker was beside them or when she was opposite. The puzzle was to find out which partial contrast constituted the next step for children who were child-centred versus speaker-centred at the earlier no contrast stage. We eventually resolved this problem by retesting some of the younger ('no contrast') children eight months later on the same task. The small number of children we managed to catch at the intermediate stage allowed us to classify the other intermediates as either child-centred or speaker-centred. Child-centred children managed to contrast *here* and *there* as long as the speaker was beside them. When she was opposite, they retained their earlier strategy of picking the toy in the near circle regardless of the instruction. The resultant pattern of right and wrong responses appears in Table 5. Speaker-centred children, on the other hand, managed to contrast *here* and *there* appropriately when the speaker was seated opposite them. But when she was beside them, they failed to make the contrast and chose the toy in the near circle as they had earlier. The pattern of right and wrong responses for these children is shown in Table 6.

Table 5
Child-centred Strategy with Partial Contrast

	Speaker beside		Speaker opposite	
Instruction:	here	there	here	there
Choice:	near circle (right)	far circle (right)	near circle (wrong)	near circle (right)

Based on Clark and Sengul (1974)

Table 6
Speaker-centred Strategy with Partial Contrast

	Speaker beside		Speaker opposite	
Instruction:	here	there	here	there
Choice:	near circle (right)	near circle (wrong)	far circle (right)	near circle (right)

Based on Clark and Sengul (1974)

The two groups at the intermediate stage of partial contrast show that there too, following on from the no contrast stage, children take different routes in working out the deictic contrast between *here* and *there*. By the time they reach the third stage, though, both groups have mastered the full adult contrast and are no longer discriminable from each other. They all do what adults do and pick the object nearest the speaker, whatever her position, when she uses *here* and the object further away when she uses *there* (Clark and Sengul, in press).

Children applied the same child-centred and speaker-centred strategies to the demonstratives as they did to the locatives. However, the contrast between the locatives was acquired before the one between the demonstratives. Of the eleven children who had mastered *here* and *there*, only five had also worked out the contrast between *this* and *that*. The remaining children were still at a no contrast or partial contrast stage for *this* and *that*, and there were no instances of children mastering these contrasts in the other order.

The contrast between *here* and *there* is mastered at around the age of five, with the contrast between the demonstratives coming in shortly afterwards. Although children may seem to have these contrasts earlier, this experiment provides a critical test because it allows children no external clues based on gesture, gaze, collocation, or context. As a result, they are forced to rely on their knowledge of the deictic words alone. Five may seem rather old for this acquisition—it is a full two years after the acquisition of the contrast between *I* and *you*—but what is crucial is that we are talking about the acquisition of the adult *deictic* contrast, as opposed to any other contrasts possible. In working out these contrasts, children again go through three general stages—first a period of no contrast, followed by one of partial contrast, followed finally by the full contrast.

Come and *go* and *bring* and *take*

Diary studies and vocabulary records suggest that most children use the verbs *come* and *go* by 2;6 or 3;0, with *bring* and *take* appearing a few months later. However, records like these provide very little information about how the verbs are used. Although mistakes are difficult to detect, as for *here* and *there*, a few have been reported by careful observers. Van der Geest (1975), for example, noted that his son Mark often used *come* where *go* would have been the appropriate verb for an adult speaker. In one such situation, Mark's mother was on the ground floor, Mark himself, aged 2;9, was on the first floor, and his father on the second floor of their house. Mark wanted to go on upstairs to the second floor but his mother thought it too dangerous:

Mother	Mark, hou je goed vast aan de leuning en kom naar beneden. ('Mark, hold tightly onto the banisters and come downstairs')
Mark	Ik hou me goed vast aan de leuning en kom naar boven. ('I hold tight onto the banisters and come upstairs')

Mark ought to have used *go* (Dutch *ga*) in lieu of *come* since he was moving away from the person he addressed. Mistakes like this are usually very difficult to detect because it is nearly always possible to imagine some circumstance under which a specific use of *come* or *go* would be appropriate. The problem is similar to that caused by shifting boundaries with *here* and *there*, and for this reason what children understand of verbs like *come* and *go* is more revealing of their hypotheses and strategies than their own uses of the verbs.

The first hypothesis that children seem to entertain about the meanings of *come* and *go* is that they mean 'move'. And even at age 4;6 or so, children seem unaware that the motion has anything to do with the speaker. Macrae (1976), for example, found that children between 3;0 and 4;10 treated *come* and *go* just like *run, jump,* and *walk*. She presented children with two dolls, one (the speaker) standing halfway up some steps, as shown in Fig. 2, and the other doing whatever the first doll said. The instructions were all of the form 'John says to Mary "Come up the steps"', and the children then moved the second doll, Mary, in the way they thought appropriate. The instructions contained one of five verbs (*come, go, run, walk* and *jump*) and either *up the steps* or *down the steps*. If children of this age understood *come*, they should move Mary from the top step down to John for *come down* and from the bottom step up to John for *come up*. With deictic *go*, on the other hand, they should move Mary away from John to the top step for *go up* and away from John to the bottom step for *go down*. Only one child, aged 4;5, stopped Mary at the speaker with *come up* and *come down*. The others treated all five verbs alike in that they ignored the speaker's position in carrying out each instruction. For four-year-olds, then, *come* and *go* mean 'move'.

Although four- and five-year olds treat *come* and *go* as if they were the same, some children may partially differentiate them on the basis of *go out* or *go away, come in* or *come here* versus *go to school*, and so on. But most four-year-olds, when asked, insist that the verbs *mean* the same thing. Five-year-olds are slightly more cautious and tend to define them in terms of set collocations, e.g. '*Come* is *come here* and *go* is *go away*'. Many of them seem to have realized that direction as well as motion is involved, but the direc-

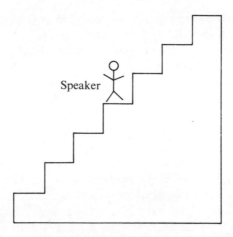

Fig. 2. Testing Deictic Contrasts: *Come* and *Go*. (Based on Macrae, 1976.) Position of the doll speaker from which the different instructions to the other doll were uttered.

tionality has yet to be tied to the speaker. One five-year-old I asked came up with a different distinction, a rather unexpected one: 'Of course they're different. *Come* begins with C and *go* with G!'

When do children begin to tie the directionality of *come* and *go* to the speaker? In order to find out, Olga Garnica and I devised several situations in which we asked children to identify the speaker or the addressee of utterances containing *come, go, bring,* and *take.* Children between 5;6 and 9;5 were presented with trios of animals, arranged facing each other, with one inside a specific location (the pig in the garden), as shown in Fig. 3. They were then given instructions like 'Which animal can say to the dog "Come into the garden"?' or 'The monkey says "Go into the garden." Which animal is he talking to?' The children had to identify the speaker in the first case (the pig, in Fig. 3) and the addressee in the second (the dog, in Fig. 3).[4] The situations were arranged so that whenever the verb *come* was used, the animal to be identified (whether speaker or addressee) was

[4] Other situations in this study involved the use of assertions about the speaker ('I'm coming/going into the garden') or about a third person ('X is coming/going into the garden'), and questions ('Can I come/go into the garden?').

inside the 'goal' (in the garden, for example), and whenever the verb *go* was used, the animal to be identified was outside the 'goal'. (The 'goal' represents the place towards which the motion is directed.) These are the choices made by adults, so if children understand the deictic contrast between *come* and *go*, they should choose an animal in the goal with *come* and one outside with *go* (see further Clark and Garnica, 1974).

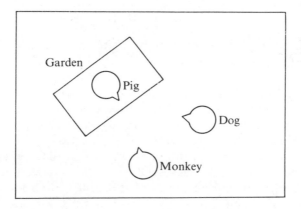

Fig. 3. Testing Deictic Contrasts: Identifying Speaker and Addressee with *Come* and *Go*. (Based on Clark and Garnica, 1974.) Positions of the three animals, all facing each other, with one inside a specific location and the other two outside facing in.

Although the children were increasingly correct as they got older, very few children under 8;6 succeeded in giving wholly adult responses. But it's impossible to see what is going on without examining each child's error-pattern in detail. These patterns suggested that children go through four stages in the acquisition of the contrast between *come* and *go*. These stages and the strategy used in each are summarized in Table 7.

At the first stage, the children treated both *come* and *go* as verbs of motion, and their strategy was to always choose the animal at the goal (e.g. the one in the garden, Fig. 3), regardless of whether they had to identify the speaker or the addressee. This strategy made it look as though the

Table 7
Strategies for Identifying Speaker and Addressee

Stage	Speaker	Addressee
1	Choose goal	Choose goal
2	Choose non-goal	Choose goal
3	a. If *come*, choose goal b. If *go*, choose non-goal	Choose goal
4	a. If *come*, choose goal b. If *go*, choose non-goal	a. If *come*, choose goal b. If *go*, choose non-goal

Based on Clark and Garnica (1974)

children were getting *come* right all the time and *go* wrong. However, the strategies used by older children made it clear that this group did not really understand the deictic nature of *come*, but got it 'right' simply as a result of their strategy.[5]

At the next stage, the children seemed to focus on the speaker and addressee and began to contrast them. Their strategy was to choose an animal outside the goal as speaker and the animal inside as addressee. Paradoxically, this strategy made the children do less well than the younger ones on *come*. They got *come* right half the time—when identifying the addressee—and wrong the other half. They also got *go* right half the time—in this case when identifying the speaker—and wrong otherwise. The data on *come*—half-right and half-wrong—show that the younger children probably did not understand *come* although they appeared to be getting it right all the time. Their strategy of choosing the animal at the goal would account for all their 'right' responses on *come* as well as all their 'wrong' ones on *go*. It is therefore more reasonable to assume that the younger children had not yet acquired the deictic meaning of *come* (see Clark, 1973, 1977).

At a third stage children worked out the appropriate choices for identifying the speaker (inside the goal with *come*, outside with *go*) but, for both verbs, continued to identify

[5] The strategy of focusing on the goal of motion also appears in much younger children learning the directional contrasts between pairs of words like *to* and *from*, *into* and *out of*, and *onto* and *off* (Macrae, 1976). In each pair, the goal-strategy makes it appear that children understand the positive terms (*to*, *into*, and *onto*) before the negative ones (*from*, *out of*, and *off*).

the animal at the goal as the addressee. As a result, they were right on *come* all the time, but right on *go* only when identifying the speaker. Logically, this stage seems to follow Stage 2 in Table 7, since the children seem to have moved to a hypothesis where they have worked out a partial contrast between *come* and *go*, a contrast that applies whenever the speaker is to be identified. The ordering of these two stages is not certain since the children did not differ significantly in age, but both groups were consistently older than children at Stage 1.

The last stage, Stage 4, corresponds to the full adult contrast. Only a few of the older children fell into this group, managing the contrast between *come* and *go* for both speaker and addressee. These children were reliably older than those at the wrong or partial contrast stages.

All the children tested for their comprehension of *come* and *go* were subsequently tested, on the same task, with *bring* and *take* ('cause to come' and 'cause to go'). The contrast between *come* and *go* was mastered before the one between *bring* and *take*, but children went through the same stages, using the same strategies, with both pairs of verbs. The causal component in *bring* and *take* seemed to add to the complexity of their pair and hence delayed acquisition of the deictic component in their meanings.

Thus, children acquiring deictic verbs also seem to go through three stages. At first they make no contrasts at all. Next they work out a partial contrast, and only after that do they arrive at the full adult contrast. These stages are marked by the use of different strategies for dealing with the verbs in the instructions. These strategies, summarized in Table 7, show how the children's hypotheses about the meanings of *come, go, bring*, and *take* change with age. At first they seem to assume that all the verbs mean 'move' and focus on the goal when asked to identify the speaker or addressee of particular utterances. Then they begin to distinguish between speaker and addressee but still make no contrast between the verbs. At the next stage, their strategy shows that they contrast *come* and *go*, and *bring* and *take*, whenever they have to identify the speaker, but not otherwise. Finally, when they come up with the adult hypothesis about the meanings of these verbs, it is reflected in their strategy for choosing speaker and addressee for each deictic verb.

The average age of the children who had worked out the full contrast for *come* and *go* was 8;8 and for *bring* and *take* it was 8;11, a long time after the acquisition of the locative and demonstrative contrasts at age five. Children may appear to have a contrast between *come* and *go* rather earlier, but unless they can use it in tasks like this where the only clues to the speaker and addressee are linguistic ones, they cannot be said to have acquired the adult *deictic* contrast. This, of course, raises the question of whether it is simply task-difficulty that makes this acquisition seem so late. The difficulty is unavoidable because the situations we used already constitute the minimal ones necessary for a test of whether children understand these deictic verbs. Moreover, the children in our study didn't show any of the usual signs of treating the task as a difficult one: their choices were always swiftly made and they were very confident, at all age levels, that they were right. In addition to this, Macrae's (1976) study as well as our own pilot work showed that four- and five-year-olds do not understand the deictic nature of these verbs at all. It may be argued that in real situations children would be able to use these terms at an earlier age than our task showed. This is unimportant to the present hypothesis as long as these contrasts are acquired *after* the other deictic contrasts. But, quite independently of this issue, the present task is important because it shows very clearly which strategies children use at different stages in the course of acquisition.

CONCLUSIONS

In this preliminary outline of the natural history of deixis, I have tried to show what goes on as children learn progressively more details about one part of language—the system of deictic contrasts. In doing this, I have argued (1) that they continually build on what they already know in forming hypotheses about language, and (2) that their strategies for using words depend on their hypotheses about the meanings. In some cases, children come up with very similar hypotheses and therefore rely on similar strategies. In others, their hypotheses differ and so they may follow different routes in working out the adult meaning.

The strategies children use can show what hypotheses are formed initially and how they are modified in the course of acquisition (Clark, 1975, in press). In this paper I have presented a preliminary account of some of these hypotheses and strategies. This account illustrates two general trends in acquisition: the centrality of the speaker, child, and goal in their hypotheses and the different routes they can take in getting to the adult meaning.

The speaker is central to the deictic terms I have been concerned with. All of them pick out particular objects in relation to the speaker. And once children have acquired the first deictic contrast, that between *I* (the speaker) and *you* (the addressee), many of them take up the notion of speaker directly in formulating their hypotheses about other deictic contrasts. For example, a number of children start off with a speaker-centred hypothesis about the meanings of *here* and *there* (Tables 4 and 6), namely that these words pick out objects near the speaker. The same is true of *this* and *that*. The speaker also emerges as central in the acquisition of deictic verbs. For example, children first worked out the contrast between *come* and *go* in relation to the speaker and only later extended the contrast to the situations affecting the addressee.

The notion of the child also plays a role in the acquisition of deixis. When children work out their first deictic contrast, the one between *I* and *you*, although most of them seem to start with a speaker-based hypothesis, some instead make the child central. Their hypothesis is that *you* always picks out the child and *I* the adult. A similar focus on the child appears in the acquisition of *here* and *there*, and *this* and *that*. Some children start out with the child-centred hypothesis that these terms pick out places and objects near the child. The questions that remain to be answered here are (1) what pushes some children to adopt one hypothesis and others another? and (2) what causes children who start with the wrong hypothesis to change it? In addition to these two questions, one might ask whether those children who focus on the speaker straightaway for *I* and *you* are the same ones who begin with a speaker-centred hypothesis about *here* and *there* and *this* and *that*. Similarly, are those children who start out with a child–adult contrast for the pronouns the same ones who start out with a child-centred hypothesis about locatives and demonstratives? As yet, there are no answers to these questions.

The third notion that appears to play a role in the acquisition of deictic contrasts is that of the goal. In working out the contrasts between *come* and *go*, and *bring* and *take*, children all seem to begin by focusing on the goal of the motion—the place towards which someone is moving. Their resultant strategy of choosing objects at the goal when asked to identify speaker or addressee has a long developmental history. Very young children have a strong perference for moving an object towards, into, or on to another—a goal-directed strategy—rather than moving an object away from, out of, or off another (Macrae, 1976). When presented with two objects, they consistently choose to place one in or on the other rather than move them apart (Clark, 1973). These preferences might also explain why, at the no contrast stage for *here* and *there*, and *this* and *that*, children choose the object *near* the speaker or child, rather than the one further away.

Notice how these strategies play a role over a very long period of time. This natural history of deixis started with children's earliest deictic gestures directed at others and followed their progress in working out the deictic contrasts between pronouns (*I* versus *you*), then locatives (*here* versus *there*), then demonstratives (*this* versus *that*), then intransitive verbs (*come* versus *go*), and finally causative verbs (*bring* versus *take*). The contrast between the demonstratives followed very shortly after the locative one, just as the contrast between the causative verbs followed very close behind the intransitive one. Deictic gestures appear at around the age of one and the successive deictic contrasts take seven or eight years to work out for a fairly limited set of contexts. The deictic system in its entirety could well take even longer to master. Yet the same notions—speaker, child, and goal—are as important to the first deictic contrasts acquired as they are to the later ones.

In brief, a natural history like this one has broad implications for the study of language acquisition. First of all, it reveals the kinds of hypotheses children may entertain about specific domains in the language being acquired. In the domain of deixis, their hypotheses centre around such notions as speaker, child, goal, and motion. Secondly, it gives an account of the specific strategies children derive from their hypotheses. In deixis, children use notions like speaker or child to come up with strategies that are speaker-centred or child-centred. And thirdly, it shows how these hypotheses and strategies determine the particular route children follow in getting to the adult meanings. For example, in the acquisition of *here* and *there*, they followed one of two routes depending on whether their initial hypothesis centred on the speaker or on the child.

The general lesson such natural histories offer is that language is never learned in isolation. In the very beginning children start off with gestures and build on the directive function of these in their first deictic words. Later on, when they acquire more complex deictic words, each set presupposes the prior acquisition of the different notions involved. For example, before children can work out the full contrast between verbs like *come* and *go*, they must know about speakers, goals, and motion. Without these notions, they would be unable to learn the adult meanings. The process of language acquisition depends crucially on cognitive development—on what children know and how they use their knowledge when they come to tackle language.

REFERENCES

AMES, L. B., 'The sense of self of nursery school children as manifested by their verbal behaviour.' *Journal of Genetic Psycology*, 81, 193–232, 1952.

ANTINUCCI, F., 'Sulla deissi.' *Lingua e Stile*, 11, 223–47, 1974.

BAIN, R., 'The self-and-other words of a child.' *American Journal of Sociology*, 41, 767–75, 1936.

BATES, E., *Language and context: The acquisition of pragmatics.* New York: Academic Press, 1976.

BATES, E., BENIGNI, L., BRETHERTON, I., CAMAIONI, L., and VOLTERRA, V., 'From gesture to the first word: On cognitive and social prerequisites.' In M. Lewis and L. Rosenblum (eds.),

Origins of behaviour: Communication and language. New York: Wiley, 1976.

BATES, E., CAMAIONI, L., and VOLTERRA, V., 'The acquisition of performatives prior to speech.' *Merrill-Palmer Quarterly*, 21, 205-26, 1975.

BLOOM, L. M., *Language development: Form and function in emerging grammars.* Cambridge, Mass.: M.I.T. Press, 1970.

BOWER, T. G. R., *Development in infancy.* San Francisco, Calif.: Freeman & Co., 1974.

BOWERMAN, M., 'Learning the structure of causative verbs: A study in the relationship of cognitive, semantic and syntactic development.' *Papers & Reports on Child Language Development* (Stanford University), 8, 142-78, 1974.

BRESSON, F., 'Remarks on genetic psycholinguistics: The acquisition of the article system in French.' In *Problèmes actuels en psycholinguistique/Current problems in psycholinguistics.* Paris: Éditions du C.N.R.S., 1974.

BRUNER, J., 'The ontogenesis of speech acts.' *Journal of Child Language*, 2, 1-19, 1975.

CARROLL, J. B., 'Determining and numerating adjectives in children's speech.' *Child Development*, 10, 215-29, 1939.

CLARK, E. V., 'Non-linguistic strategies and the acquisition of word meanings.' *Cognition*, 2, 161-82, 1973.

CLARK, E. V., 'Normal states and evaluative viewpoints.' *Language*, 50, 316-32, 1974.

CLARK, E. V., 'Knowledge, context, and strategy in the acquisition of meaning.' In D. P. Dato (ed.), *Georgetown University Round Table on Languages and Linguistics 1975.* Washington D.C.: Georgetown University Press, 1975.

CLARK, E. V., 'Strategies and the mapping problem in first language acquisition.' In J. Macnamara (ed.), *Language learning and thought.* New York: Academic Press, 1977.

CLARK, E. V. and GARNICA, O. K., 'Is he coming or going? On the acquisition of deictic verbs.' *Journal of Verbal Learning & Verbal Behaviour*, 13, 556-72, 1974.

CLARK, E. V. and SENGUL, C. J., 'Deictic contrasts in language acquisition.' Paper presented at the Annual Meeting of the Linguistic Society of America, New York City, December 1974.

CLARK, E. V. and SENGUL, C. J., Strategies in the acquisition of deixis' *Journal of Child Language*, in press.

COLLIS, G. M., 'Visual co-orientation and maternal speech.' In H. R. Schaffer (ed.), *Studies in mother–infant interaction: The Loch Lomond Syposium.* London: Academic Press, 1977.

COOLEY, C. H., 'A study of the early use of self-words by a child.' *Psychological Review*, 15, 339-57, 1908.

DE LAGUNA, G. A., *Speech: Its function and development.* New Haven, Conn.: Yale University Press, 1927.

ESCALONA, S. K., 'Basic modes of social interaction: Their emergence and patterning during the first two years of life.' *Merrill-Palmer Quarterly*, 19, 205–32, 1973.

FILLMORE, C. J., 'Deictic categories in the semantics of *Come.*' *Foundations of Language*, 2, 219–27, 1966.

FILLMORE, C. J., 'Lectures on deixis'. Unpublished MSS., Summer Program in Linguistics, University of California at Santa Cruz, 1971.

FOULKE, K. and STINCHFIELD, S. M., 'The speech development of four infants under two years of age.' *Journal of Genetic Psychology*, 36, 140–71, 1929.

FREI, H., 'Systèmes de déictiques.' *Acta Linguistica*, 4, 111–29, 1944.

GARNICA, O. K., 'Non-verbal concomitants of language input to children: Clues to meaning.' Paper presented at the Third International Child Language Symposium, University of London, September 1975.

GHEORGOV, I. A., 'Die ersten Anfänge des sprachlichen Ausdrucks für das Selbstbewusstsein bei Kindern.' *Achive für gesamte Psychologie*, 5, 329–404, 1905.

GRANT, J. R., 'A child's vocabulary and its growth.' *Pedagogical Seminary*, 22, 183–203, 1915.

GRIFFITHS, P., '*That there* deixis I: *that.*' Unpublished paper, University of York, 1974.

HALLIDAY, M. A. K., *Learning how to mean: Explorations in the development of language.* London: Arnold, 1975.

HUXLEY, R., 'The development of the correct use of subject personal pronouns in two children.' In G. B. Flores d'Arcais & W. J. M. Levelt (eds.), *Advances in psycholinguistics.* Amsterdam: North-Holland Publishing Co., 1970.

JESPERSEN, O., *Language, its nature, development, and origin.* London: Allen & Unwin, 1922.

KURYLOWICZ, J., *The inflectional categories of Indo-European.* Heidelberg: Carl Winter Universitätsverlag, 1964.

LEMPERS, J., FLAVELL, E. L., and FLAVELL, J. H., *The development in very young children of tacit knowledge concerning visual perception.* Genetic Psychology Monographs, 95, 3–53, 1977.

LEOPOLD, W. F., *Speech development of a bilingual child.* (4 vols.) Evanston, Ill.: Northwestern University Press, 1949.

LINDNER, G., *Aus dem Naturgarten der Kindersprache.* Leipzig: Grieben, 1898.

LYONS, J., 'Deixis as the source of reference.' In E. L. Keenan (ed.), *Formal semantics of natural language.* London: Cambridge University Press, 1975.

MACRAE, A. J., 'Meaning relations in language development: A study of some converse pairs and directional opposites.' Unpublished Ph.D. dissertation, University of Edinburgh, 1976.

MARATSOS, M. P., *The use of definite and indefinite reference in young children.* London: Cambridge University Press, 1976.

MURPHY, C. M. and MESSER, D. J., 'Mothers, infants, and pointing: A study of gesture.' In H. R. Schaffer (ed.), *Studies in mother-infant interaction.* London: Academic Press, 1977.

NELSON, K., *Structure and strategy in learning how to talk. Monographs of the Society for Research in Child Development*, 38 (Serial No. 149), 1973.

NICE, M. M., 'The development of a child's vocabulary in relation to environment.' *Pedagogical Seminary*, 22, 35–64, 1915.

PIAGET, J., *The construction of reality in the child*. New York: Basic Books, 1954.

RHEINGOLD, H., 'Sharing at an early age.' Presidential address, Division 7, Annual Meeting of the American Psychological Association, Montreal, September 1973.

RODGON, M., 'Overt action ᴗ ᴗᴐ semantic expression of action in early one- and two-word utterances.' Paper presented at the Psychology of Language Conference, University of Stirling, June 1976.

SANCHES, M., 'Features in the acquisition of Japanese.' Unpublished Ph.D. dissertation, Stanford University, 1968.

SAVIC, S., 'One form of imitation and creation in child speech among young children.' *Pedagogy* (Belgrade), 3, 147–60, 1974.

SEARLE, J. R., *Speech acts*. London: Cambridge University Press, 1969.

SHARPLESS, E. A., 'Children's acquisition of personal pronouns.' Unpublished Ph.D. dissertation, Columbia University, 1974.

SHATZ, M., 'The comprehension of indirect directives: Can two-year-olds shut the door?' Paper presented at the Summer Meeting of the Linguistic Society of America, Amherst, Mass., July 1974.

SHIPLEY, E. F. and SHIPLEY, T. E., 'Quaker children's use of *Thee*: A relational analysis.' *Journal of Verbal Learning & Verbal Behaviour*, 8, 112–17, 1969.

SNYDER, A. D., 'Notes on the talk of a two-and-a-half year old boy.' *Pedagogical Seminary*, 21, 412–24, 1914.

SULLY, J., *Studies of Childhood*. New York, Appleton, 1896.

THORNE, J. P., 'On the notion "definite."' *Foundations of Language*, 8, 562–8, 1972.

THORNE, J. P., 'Notes on "Notes on 'On the notion "definite"'".' *Foundations of Language*, 11, 111–14, 1974.

TRAUGOTT, E. C., 'Spatial expressions of tense and temporal sequencing: A contribution to the study of semantic fields.' *Semiotica*, 15, 207–30, 1975.

VAN DER GEEST, T., *Evaluation of theories on child grammars*. The Hague: Mouton, 1974.

VAN DER GEEST, T., *Some aspects of communicative competence and their implications for language acquisition*. Amsterdam: Van Gorcum, 1975.

WARDEN, D. A., 'The influence of context on children's use of identifying expressions and references.' *British Journal of Psychology*, 67, 101–12, 1976.

WEIR, R. H., *Language in the crib*. The Hague: Mouton, 1962.

WERNER, H. and KAPLAN, B., *Symbol formation*. New York: Wiley, 1963.

5 New Currents in Genetic Epistemology and Developmental Psychology[1]

BÄRBEL INHELDER

Genetic epistemology and developmental psychology inform Piaget's theory and the work of the Genevan school as a whole. For Piaget, the problems are epistemological ones, and genetic epistemology is the method he has chosen to study them. However, the relation between epistemology and psychology is far more than a superficial link between the object of a scientific study and its method. There is a deep continuity and a fertile interaction between epistemological constructions, the structural analysis of the fundamental categories of thought, and the study of the discovery strategies constructed by the individual subject. The object of my own most recent research concerns these discovery strategies and I feel that such a study of the 'psychological subject' complements that of the 'epistemic subject'.

Piaget's research has had a strong interdisciplinary character: he sets out to solve epistemological problems by combining the developmental approach with critical analyses of the history of science and by using models based on logic, mathematics and biologically founded cybernetics. This multidimensional approach leads to a remarkably broad view of the laws and mechanisms of cognitive development. The genesis of knowledge, the productivity of the human mind, and its manifold inventions and discoveries are the central themes of Piaget's conceptual system which, though highly consistent, is nevertheless in constant evolution. Such a combination of conservation and transformation of structures is a prominent feature of Piaget's theory, which is essentially

[1] The work reported here was partially supported by the Ford Foundation Fund and by the Swiss National Fund for Scientific Research.

biological. Piaget's constructivist view of development grows directly out of his biological view of the nature of intelligence: self-organizing and self-regulating mechanisms form the continuity between organic functioning and cognitive functioning.

In the work of my own research team, the constructivist aspect of Piaget's theory is the most important, and I will start with a brief outline of its features.

The term 'constructivist' was chosen since knowledge is considered to be neither pre-formed in the object (empiricism) nor in the subject (nativism) but as resulting from progressive construction: reality is continuously restructured through the subject's own activities.

To say that knowledge depends on the subject's activities does not mean that it is innate: rather it is precisely these very activities that create new structures and new forms of organization. For example, it is clear that during a certain period children see no necessity in the deduction $A > B$, $B > C : A > C$—even if they manage empirically to seriate sticks of various lengths. But on the basis of their activities, the operational notion of seriation is constructed, and it is this which gives rise to the logical necessity of the relationship. While current studies of infants, at Oxford as well as at Edinburgh, have shown a variety of innate competencies, these results provide, it is true, certain arguments in favour of nativism and are used by some as evidence against the constructivist interpretation. Yet, between such early behaviour and analogous behaviour patterns that arise some months later, there must be a process of reconstruction and not a simple and direct continuity as often seems to be supposed by generalized nativist theory.

From our point of view, each new stage in cognitive development is characterized by new creations which, in turn, open up new possibilities. When a structure is comparatively weak, the possibilities are comparatively few, but the more powerful the structure, the greater the number of possibilities.

This principle is illustrated not only by the child's cognitive development but also by the history of mathematics and physics. Piaget is at present working with the physicist and historian of sciences, Rolando Garcia, to elucidate the mechanisms that account for both the psychogenetic structuration of intelligence and the historical development of theories in mathematics and physics. The levels of abstraction are obviously quite different among children and among scientists. Yet one finds surprising analogies between children's ways of explaining natural phenomena and the thinking about mechanics in Antiquity and the Middle Ages, especially when comparing children's explanations of the transmission of movement and other physical phenomena and the thinking about mechanics in Antiquity and the Middle Ages, especially when comparing children's explanations of the transmission of movement and other physical phenomena with specific passages in Buridan or Oresme, the great masters of the fourteenth century. However, these analogies may be considered as bearing on the content of knowledge rather than on the mechanisms of its construction. Of much greater interest are the parallels they found in the construction of knowledge, parallels that extend not only to the structures which characterize certain stages of development, but even to the modes of transition from one structure to another.

For example, in the history of geometry before our century, one may distinguish three stages characterized by (a) the geometry of the Greeks and its evolution up to the end of the eighteenth century, (b) projective geometry (Poncelet, Chasles), and (c) the 'global' conception of geometry introduced by Klein. The development of descriptive geometry by Descartes and Fermat, and of calculus, provided the instruments for the transition from (a) to (b); and group theory for the transition from (b) to (c). Here one finds a similarity with the stages Piaget described in children as 'intrafigural', 'interfigural', and 'transfigural'. The epistemological analysis of those differences shows profound reasons for this parallelism and has demonstrated beyond expectation the fertility of psychogenetic research for understanding the evolution of scientific thought.

This constructivist approach to epistemological problems first gave rise to a series of studies on basic cognitive categories (space, time, causality, etc.), in which laws governing cognitive development were discovered. The universality of the sequence of developmental periods, each marking the completion of the preceding one and giving rise to the new possibilities of the next, reflects their intrinsic necessity. However, it should not be forgotten that this necessity may be very different from that which is inherent in the thought of the psychologist observer. The much-discussed question of the relations between observer and observed arises in a particularly acute form when it comes to cognitive structures and their development. When developmental psychologists try to reconstruct the elaboration of certain forms of knowledge in terms of interactions between subject and object, they sooner or later observe coherent action-systems that combine with one another in certain specific ways and which Piaget analysed in terms of structures.

All too often, it is forgotten that these systems are not always conceptualized by the subjects themselves: the structures account for what the subjects can do, but no reflection by the subject on his own operatory constructions is presupposed.

The structure concept has given rise to many controversies. For some authors, structures are no more than logico-mathematical models chosen by the observer for their heuristic value; for others, like Piaget, they also correspond to systems that underly the subject's activities. I personally prefer to consider them in terms of their varying degrees of congruence with psychological reality. It seems to me that even psychologists who mistrust structuralism, because they fear an unwarranted realistic interpretation, or because of methodological caution, would admit that a structuralist approach often allows upper and lower limits to be placed on a subject's capacity for certain problems and at certain developmental levels. Above all, a structuralist description, since it can show the similarity between systems, often suggests links between behaviours that at first may appear unconnected.

Yet the structural aspect of knowledge which determines the hierarchical order of its successive forms cannot, on its own, account for the dynamics of progress, which is after all of central concern to developmental psychologists. The motor of such progress is to be sought, according to Piaget, in regulatory mechanisms leading to augmentative re-equilibrations. Thus, in a series of studies on the relations between learning and structures of knowledge, we studied the functional processes of developmental dynamics. More particularly, the transitions that characterize the passage from one level to the next were analyzed, as well as the links between different systems of operatory schemes, each of which has its own pace of development. We supposed that it was precisely the conflict between schemes of different levels that generated a disequilibrium. The resulting conflicts and contradictions could in turn be supposed to put in motion the processes that would lead to new solutions.

So as to be able to follow the unfolding of such processes, we constructed learning procedures (Inholder, Sinclair, Bouet, 1974) in which the interaction with a real situation and the dialectics of contradiction proved essential moments in the process of thought. The subject's behaviour during several successive learning sessions provided us with a kind of micro-genesis, that is to say, a compression in time, of a process that would take much longer without such specially designed occasions for learning. The nature of the changes in behaviour noted during the learning sessions provides a key to the dynamics of progress.

One of the learning studies dealt with the concept of conservation of quantities. A frame was constructed consisting of a vertical column to which two horizontal bars were attached, on a flat base; to each of these, two glasses were fixed (Fig. 1). The top and the middle glasses had taps at the bottom, so that liquid would flow from A to B to C and from A' to B' to C'. The two top glasses (A and A') and the two bottom glasses (C and C') were identical in shape and size, and remained fixed during the experiment, but glasses B and B' could be replaced by either a narrower glass (N), or a wider one. After a period of free play during which the child observed the flow from A to C and A' to C', glass B' was replaced by the narrower glass.

The child was asked to pour an equal amount of liquid into A and A', and after he had done this carefully, he was asked to open the tap of A and to let all the liquid flow into B. Then came the difficult request: he has to open the tap

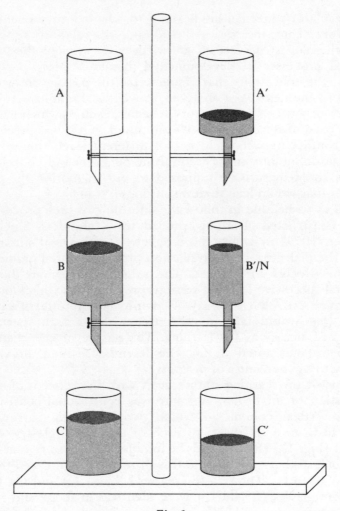

Fig. 1

of A' and let the liquid flow down into N 'so that there will be just as much liquid in B as in N'. Usually, a child who has not yet acquired the concept of conservation will judge that there is 'more to drink' whenever the liquid level is higher, ignorning possible differences in the shape of the glasses, and ignoring the fact (which he has clearly observed) that nothing has been added or taken away when the liquid was allowed to run from two identical glasses whose content he has judged to be of equal quantity. Such a child will carefully close the tap as soon as the level of the liquid in N reaches that of the liquid in B, thus leaving some liquid in A' whereas A is totally empty. After the child has affirmed that there is just as much to drink in B and N, he is asked to predict whether there will also be the same amount to drink in C and C' if the liquid is run into the bottom glasses. Without paying any attention to the liquid left in A', children of this stage are convinced that all will be well, and are very surprised when they see it is not. At this point, they suddenly seem to 'perceive' the liquid left in A' and propose to let it flow down too.

All the subjects correctly observed the equality or difference of the levels, but not all of them were capable of benefiting from this observation to arrive at the correct solution for the B and N glasses. It is one thing to find one's prediction contradicted by reality, and quite another to be able to become aware of the contradiction in one's own reasoning. Surprise and interest when confronted with unexpected phenomena is only a beginning: the next step implies reflection on one's own thinking and a capacity of drawing inferences from what has been observed. Interestingly, it was mainly those subjects that during the pre-test had shown signs of being more advanced who made progress during the training sessions in the sense that their post-tests showed a stable acquisition.

In all our learning studies we obtained authentic progress with a relatively large number of subjects. Development was accelerated in the experimental group in comparison with the control group, and acquisitions proved to be stable. This result makes it very clear that the acquisition of a concept such as conservation is not simply due to maturation, but to the interaction between the subject's assimilatory schemes and the specific experiences provided by the environment.

Since the Genevan psychogenetic view of development, opposed as it is to any empiricist position, is often confused with maturationist theory, the positive results of our learning studies should be stressed. However, another point also needs stressing: development was accelerated through the learning procedures, but it was not modified. No deviations from the known course of cognitive progress were noted and the acceleration was closely linked to small differences in the subject's competences in the pre-tests. Those subjects who were capable of benefitting from the learning situations benefitted more and more as the sessions went on. Each new contribution from the environment is apparently more rapidly assimilated when more extensive networks of schemes already exist.

These learning studies, like all Genevan researches until very recently focused on the construction of cognitive operations, and thus on the comprehension of reality. Our current research, by contrast, is focused on the processes of invention or discovery when the subject is searching for a solution to a specific problem. This of course does not mean that we are pursuing a totally different direction of research: discovery and invention clearly have their place in the child's progress of comprehension (or maybe one should speak of rediscoveries of what scientific thought has already achieved). Reciprocally, in every discovery process the subject advances in comprehension.

The structural approach to cognition was focused on the most general or even universal aspect of the growth of knowledge, whereas the processes of invention for discovery give rise to context-bound procedures that may vary with the individual and the situation.

For the study of the general structural aspect, biological and mathematical models are probably more suitable, whereas for analysing individual procedures of discovery and invention procedural models derived from artifical intelligence research are more useful.

The study of such procedures will, it is hoped, go beyond the individual and lead to general laws of functioning. The procedural aspects of cognitive functioning cannot be dissociated from the meaning the child attributes to the ways and means he chooses to attain his goals, nor from the interpretative network he constructs in dealing with his still very limited universe. By 'interpretative network' is meant the systems of representation that direct the child's attention without his necessarily being capable of becoming aware of these systems or of conceptualizing them.

Since we are interested in goal-oriented procedures, we

need situations in which the child's actions allow us to infer his thought processes. The child is therefore given a goal that can be attained only through a concatenation of actions. The observer should intervene as little as possible, so as not to interrupt or disrupt the child's spontaneous activity. Only the experimental situation itself determines the limits of this activity. Certain parts of the child's activity appear crucial for understanding the strategies and means chosen by the child to solve the problem; these moments will be analysed in detail. A few examples follow.

A clear example of an experimental situation that fulfils our methodological requirements is the following (Blauchet, 1977). The child is given eight balls with strings, a collection of other strings with small clips, and a number of rods (of three different lengths) and is asked to construct a suspended mobile in which (a) all rods are horizontal, (b) all balls are used, (c) all bars have strings at their extremities (Fig. 2).

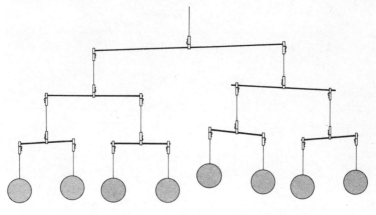

Fig. 2

The typical solution consists in a symmetrical multistage mobile. To succeed in this task, the child has to work out an understanding of the possible relationship between parts of the system and the whole, e.g. he has to realize that each modification of the suspension point results in a disequilibrium of a part of the system (and only of that part); Fig. 3(a). Each addition or elimination of a ball results in a dis-

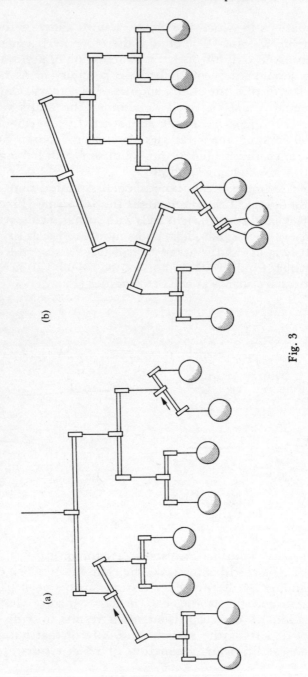

Fig. 3

equilibrium not only of the particular sub-system, but also in those other sub-systems that are themselves linked both to the point of suspension of the whole mobile and to the modified part; sub-systems that are independent of this link remain intact (Fig. 3b).

In another experiment (Karmiloff-Smith and Inhelder, 1975), children were asked to 'balance so that they do not fall' a variety of wooden bars across a metal rod fixed to a base (Fig. 4). The bars were either symmetrical in appearance and in weight distribution, or were conspicuously heavier at one end, or were invisibly weighted by the

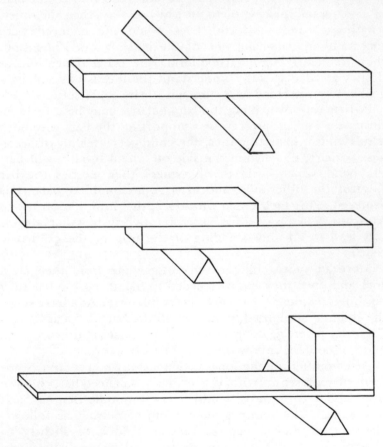

Fig. 4

insertion of a metal block at one end; yet others, if they were to balance, called for the use of counterweights, which were available to the children. Sixty-seven children aged 4½ to 9½ years took part in the experiment.

Many of the youngest children started by placing a bar haphazardly on the metal rod; when it did not remain in balance they would start again and press down hard on top of the bar with their fingers. As the block kept on falling, the children gradually discovered that the object had properties independent of their actions on it. From pursuing the goal of balancing they went over to the sub-goal of discovering the properties of the object. These children explored the bars in great detail, placing them upright one way, then the other, lengthwise, and so forth. Even when the children were successful in balancing one of the bars on one dimension, they frequently went on exploring the other dimensions as if they needed to fully understand the means of reaching a goal before returning to the pursuit of the goal itself.

A first way of making the bars balance may be called sensorimotor and proprioceptive: supporting the bars with both hands under the extremities, the child gets a feeling of heaviness which will tell him the side on which the bar will fall: the hand which feels the heaviness then pushes the bar towards the other side, and after some fumbling balance is achieved. This tactile and proprioceptive information-taking constitutes, in a way, a first interpretative system that later on will lead to an understanding of the role of the geometric centre.

More advanced children did not deviate from their main goal and once they had succeeded in balancing the bar they no longer explored it in any observable way. At a later stage, the children attempted to balance all the bars on their longest flat side, reverting to exploration and pushing down on the point of contact only with some difficult items.

After opting for the longest dimension and retaining some form of representation of a previously balanced bar, children from about 6 onwards would 'try the middle first . . . half way along'. The action sequence ran somewhat as follows: place at geometric centre, release hold very slightly to observe result, correct very slightly, correct a little more, return to geometric centre, repeat until balance is achieved. The frequent returns to the geometric centre are like a prelude to the next stage in which the geometric idea becomes so strong as to prevent many children from balancing bars they previously were successful with. They systematically place bars at the geometric centre and are most surprised when there is disequilibrium: 'Hey, what's gone wrong with this one? It worked before.' And they persist in trying to apply their theory with only minor corrective shifts as if they knew nothing of the sensori-motor approach that previously had proved adequate. Yet it is enough to ask them to close their eyes for them to resort once more to the feel of the balance; but when they open their eyes they resolutely place the bar back again on its geometric centre.

These children apparently have constructed an interpretative network, according to which all bars balance on their geometric centre. This theory, evidenced in the actions, was actually given expression by one of the children who said: 'The bars always balance when you put them on the middle.' Though it is often seen not to work, this theory-in-action is extremely persistent, and is only very gradually, often almost reluctantly, abandoned for an approach (among the eight to nine year olds) that takes both shape and weight into account. Typically, these children would pause before each item, roughly assess the weight distribution by lifting it, infer the probable point of balance and then place the bar immediately very close to his point without first attempting to balance at the geometric centre.

How does the symmetrical theory-in-action come to be abandoned or integrated into a more general theory? Three interdependent reasons may explain the strategies of the most advanced children. The first has to do with their general progress in understanding the physical world: the child realizes that for purposes of balance there is a relation between weight and length. The second is that the child becomes increasingly sensitive to the contradictions between theory and reality, while at the same time seeming to note a certain regularity among the exceptions; as one of them put it: 'It's always the opposite of what I think.' The third has to do with the child's increasing capacity to combine several modes of evaluation (tactile and proprioceptive, visual, conceptual, etc.) to form a more general system of interpretation: from this stage onwards he will consider equilibrium at the geometrical centre to be only one particular case among others.

The meaning the child attributes to what might be called the responses of the object appears to vary according to whether he is primarily oriented towards the set goal or towards comprehension (like conceiving a theory, etc.). As long as he pursued success pure and simple, that is to say perfect balance, only the positive result matters and incites him to repeat his actions. Gradually, however, his failures lead him to ask how balance can be achieved, or what means are available for this purpose, which thus leads him to explore the properties of the objects themselves. It is as if he were constructing a theory to account first of all for the regularity inherent in his successes, and only after he is completely convinced by the theory does he realize that his failures are not just exceptions to the rule but in turn obey other regularities.

In a further experiment (Inhelder, Ackermann-Valladao, *et al.*, 1976), children were asked to link two or three given points on a square grid by 'roads' made up of simple geometric shapes. Here I would like to take a small episode and describe the successive actions of one child of 6½ years (Fig. 5).

On a grid divided into 25 equal small squares, two or three toy houses are placed at the middle of the adjacent sides. On a number of cardboard squares of a size equal to the grid-squares are drawn either straight lines bisecting the square, or L-shaped lines or T-shaped lines. The child is asked to build a road that leads from house A to house B, and then to build a road leading from A to both B and to C, a house placed in the middle of the side opposite B. Subsequently there were many even more difficult tasks to perform.

As soon as the first instruction was given, the child put his hand on an L square; then he took two I-squares, put them in a straight line in the two squares in front of A, took the L-square, placed it correctly towards B, and used two more I-squares to reach B. There were no hesitation pauses,

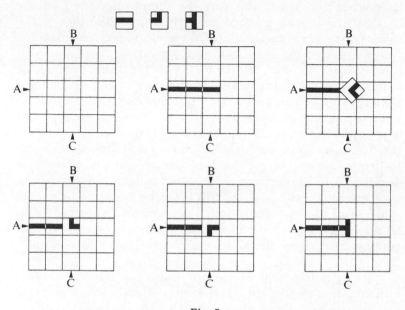

Fig. 5

and no fumbling movements when the L-shape had to be used; in fact, placing his hand immediately on this particular element, the child showed that he had understood its essential role before any construction had taken place.

The second situation proved far more difficult. Before taking any small squares, the child sketched with his forefinger, above the grid, two intersecting lines at right angles—a sort of prefiguration of the end result. Then he took three I-squares and placed them in a straight line in front of A. He noticed that this line went beyond the point where his road would have to make a turn to go towards B, and took away the third I-square. He hesitated, looked over the various elements at his disposal, took an L-square, turned it around on the table outside the grid, and finally placed it at the end of his two I-squares, so that the two branches pointed towards the two corners of the grid on the opposite side of A. In this way he appeared to mark a double branching of his straight road, one part going in the direction of B and the other in the direction of C; but he realized that neither B nor

C could be reached in this way. He then turned the L-square so that one branch pointed towards B and the other to the side of the square opposite A (it was no longer linked to the straight part of the road leading from A); he then rotated it through 90° so that one branch pointed towards C (once again, it was no longer linked to the part of the road he had already built). The child then put his hand on another I-element, probably with the idea of closing the gap, but before placing it on the grid he had another idea and turned the L-square again through 90°, so that it linked with the I-squares. After rotating the L-square several times more, he decided to finish the road with two I-squares linking A to C, thus reaching a sub-goal. At this point he appeared to see the solution all of a sudden, took a T-square, which corresponded to the figure he had sketched with his finger right in the beginning, took away the L-square, and finished the road up to B.

The figurative representation indicated that the child's initial gesture clearly did not lead him directly to the solution of the problem. Once again, the child spent some time exploring before he became aware of the 'meaning' of the different elements he had at his disposal. The L-square 'means' only one change in direction; the T-square two. For the child, the T-square apparently has two values that cannot be immediately co-ordinated: a value *per se* as a certain shape, and a transformational value when combined with other elements. The exploratory phase allows him to go from one value to the other, and only after he has mastered this aspect of the problem does he return to the initial goal. Just as in the last experiment discussed, an interruption in goal-directed behaviour takes place, during which the object's properties are apprehended so that the pertinent features can later be used for solving the problem.

It is certainly too early to draw far-reaching conclusions from our current research, of which I have given you some examples. The studies of thought in action called for new methods, for the kinds of situation that allow close observation of the procedures used by the individual subject and of the specific role he attributes to the means he chooses to reach his goal.

Earlier studies were aimed at understanding the capacities and potentialities of children at different levels of development. Our new research is focused on the way the child puts his cognitive competence to use in solving a particular problem. This orientation brings us closer to the work done in artificial intelligence, though at this stage in research no attempt is made to describe the subject's activities as computer procedures in the strict sense. Rather it is the relation between the child's plans and actions, as well as his view and understanding of the world, that we wish to grasp. The examples given appear to show the interdependence between the child's strategies for solving a problem and his understanding of reality that forms the background to his actions.

This postulated interdependence does not mean that the procedures invented or used by the child are directly derived from his already organized stock of schemes, i.e. from his cognitive structures. We hypothesize that there are several different levels of 'knowing' which lead the child to a choice of discovery or construction procedures. In the first place there is the stock of already organized knowledge, derived from the functioning of the most general schemes; this general knowledge bears on understanding reality rather than on discovery or invention. In the second place, there are the child's goal-directed procedures, chosen to deal directly with a particular problem. Construction procedures can start from opposite poles: first there is a kind of natural order that constructs from 'the bottom upwards', and order originating from the use of particular means; second, there is an inverse order, from 'the top down', that originates from the desired result of the actions. These two orders have to be reconciled, and the child's attempts to do this give rise to strategies that are repeatable and transferable. The psychological problem, therefore, is that of defining the conditions for success, i.e. the adjustment of the means to the end, which in turn can become the means for reaching new ends. This process of strategy-building should, of course, not be seen as divorced from the fundamental search for understanding; rather, the crucial question is that of the interaction between the two.

REFERENCES

BLANCHET, A., 'La construction et l'équilibre du mobile. Problèmes et méthodes.' *Archives de Psychologie,* xlv, no. 173, pp. 29–52, 1977.

INHELDER, B., SINCLAIR, H., BOVET, M., *Learning and the Development of Cognition.* Cambridge: Harvard University Press, London: Routledge and Kegan Paul, 1974.

INHELDER, B., ACKERMANN-VALLADAO, E., *et al.,* 'Des structures cognitives aux procédures de découverte Esquisse de recherches en cours.' *Archives de Psychologie,* xliv, no. 171, pp. 57–72, 1976.

KARMILOFF-SMITH, A. and INHELDER, B., 'If you want to get ahead, get a theory.' *Cognition* 3 (3), pp. 195–212, 1975.

PIAGET, J. and GARCIA, R., 'Méchanismes communs entre la psychogènese et l'histoire des sciences.' In preparation.

6 *Nursery Needs and Choices*

JACK TIZARD

Today's decisions to cut back the expansion of nursery services for young children are being presented—and very largely accepted—as based on economic grounds. They are, however, in a deeper sense, political—as the rescue of the motor-car industry and the continuing support of Concorde should remind us. Even if we confine ourselves to the allocation of resources within the education budget, we could, as is being done in France, decide to expand our nursery services and cut back instead on higher education if we chose. Unfortunately in Britain there is not to be expansion: the next few years are to see a rediscovered enthusiasm for low-cost services, for selection and means-tested provision, for child minding, for the Nixon doctrine of not having the State provide what people can provide for themselves, for cuts both in the quality and the amount of public provision we make for the education and day care of young children. Only if by any chance the supply of teachers, or nurses, or women police, or doctors, or factory workers should once again prove insufficient to meet demand, will reasons be found as to why it is right for society to provide day care for some young mothers, in order that they can work in the national interest, while it is irresponsible of other young mothers to want to 'abandon' their children or dilute the joys of motherhood.

This then, I suppose, is as bad or as good a time as any to restate the case for comprehensive nursery services, forming part of a comprehensive family policy for parents and children. In doing so I shall draw very largely upon a review of the issues undertaken with my colleagues Peter Moss and

Jane Perry (Tizard, Moss, Perry, 1976) and on current work
in the Thomas Coram Research Unit.

WE HAVE BEEN HERE BEFORE

The history of nursery services during the last century has
been one of promises of expansion followed by periods of
contraction before the promises could be redeemed in more
than token fashion. Between 1871 and 1900, and certainly
not as a result of any conscious policy on the part of government, the proportion of three- and four-year-old children in
ordinary elementary schools actually rose from 24·2 to 43·1
per cent of the age group. These were children of working-
class parents; for middle-class children, whose parents made
virtually no use of the public sector of education, day care
was provided, in part at least, by nannies—of whom there
may have been as many as half a million in England before
the First World War (Gathorne-Hardy, 1972). Since the
proportion of married women in employment probably
declined in the last three decades of the nineteenth century,
the rise in the numbers of young children in school was due
simply to the growing availability of places. Parents wanted
their children to go. A survey carried out by the NSPCC for
the 1908 Consultative Committee on School Attendance
showed that of 479 working-class parents of young children
80 per cent were in favour of their children attending school.
The reasons were mixed, but the Society reported that 'it
is clear that (there were) no divisions of views between better
and worse classes of parents.' The same is true today.

Government decisions taken in 1905 to allow local education authorities to refuse entry to children under the age of
five stifled the development of nursery services for sixty
years, though during the Second World War in particular
the demand for female labour led to an expansion both in
numbers of children under five (to about 70,000) in day nurseries, and to about twice that number in educational establishments by the end of the war. The setting-up of nurseries
didn't, as a matter of fact, result in a great net gain in woman
power; but it seemed a good and patriotic thing to do, and
it received much encouragement and financial support from
central government (Ferguson and Fitzgerald, 1954).

Following the Second World War, as everyone knows, there was yet another freeze on pre-school expansion: this despite the duty laid upon local education authorities under the 1944 Education Act to 'have regard to the need for securing that provision is made for pupils who have not attained the age of five years' either in nursery schools or nursery classes. Despite too the duty laid upon local health authorities under the National Health Service Act of 1946 to 'make arrangements for the care . . . of children who are not attending primary schools maintained by the local authority'. Once again, it seemed, there were too many other priorities. And even in 1960, when LEAs and LHAs, having surmounted their worst problems of post-war expansion, were beginning to expand their nursery services, the government .declined to sanction it—though four years later they permitted and indeed encouraged local authorities to provide places in nursery schools and day nurseries for teachers and nurses returning to work while their children were still young, while still maintaining a general prescription on expansion otherwise.

However, in 1967 the Plowden Report recommended that nursery education, mostly part-time, should be made available for 50 per cent of three-year-olds and 90 per cent of four-year-olds. The recommendations were broadly accepted by the government in 1972; they began to be implemented locally and received central backing, especially after 1973. But now expansion has virtually ground to a halt, and the next year or two promise very little.

The expansion in provision during the last few years has, however, been considerable. In mid-1974 about one-third (32 per cent) of all children aged 0–4 were getting some sort of day care, including part-time play group attendance, according to the first results of a national survey of day care use and preferences carried out by the Social Survey Division of the Office of Population Censuses and Surveys (Bone, 1976).

As we see from the table, the proportion of children receiving day care services outside their own homes rises steadily with age: only 4 per cent of infants and 8 per cent of one-year-olds, but 19 per cent of two-year-olds, 47 per cent of threes and 72 per cent of fours are in school, or at a play-

Table 1
Types of day care used by children according to age
(OPCS Survey, 1974)

Age of Children

Types of day care	Under 1 year	1–2 years	2–3 years	3–4 years	4–5 years	All ages 0–4
Playgroup	1	3	13	34	35	18
Nursery/primary school	–	–	1	9	33	9
Day nursery or crèche	–	2	2	4	3	3
Child minder	2	3	3	3	3	3
Total receiving day care	4	8	19	47	72	32
Total % (approx.)	100	100	100	100	100	100

group, or day nursery or crèche, or with a child minder.

Today the most commonly used form of day care is the play group, used by one-third of all three- and four-year-olds, and the primary school or nursery school (mainly the former) used by 9 per cent of three-year-olds and one-third of four-year-olds. Other kinds of day care make only a minor contribution to services.

WHAT DO PARENTS WANT?

There are nursery ideologies which influence government in its view about how much nursery provision should receive support from the public purse. However, one determinant that might be expected to have had a greater influence than it has up to now is demand: the desire of parents to send their children to some form of day care. At the turn of the century, as I mentioned, 43 per cent of parents sent their three- and four-year-old children to what were then called baby classes in elementary schools, and perhaps as many as 80 per cent wished to do so. Seventy-five years later only 21 per cent of three- and four-year-olds were in educational establishments, though if we include play groups the proportions are larger, especially of four-year-olds. Even so, they fall far short of parental desires, as we shall see.

Now until quite recently, with the exception of a few *ad*

hoc inquiries such as the 1908 survey by the NSPCC, no one ever thought to ask the parents what *they* wanted for their children. The OPCS survey did, however, do just this. Table 2 presents the findings, showing the proportions both of those who were using day care and of those who desired it.

Table 2
Parental Desire for Day care, by age of children
(OPCS Survey, 1974)

Age of child

	Under 1 year	1–2 years	2–3 years	3–4 years	4–5 years	*All ages*
Day care used	4	8	19	47	72	32
Not used but desired	16	34	53	40	19	33
Total desiring day care	20	41	72	87	91	64

The proportion desiring some form of day care service is already 20 per cent for infants and 41 per cent for one-year-olds; it rises to 72 per cent for two-year-olds and to about 90 per cent for children aged three and four. To judge from these figures the extent of unmet demand is enormous.

There is good evidence that one can rely on the findings of this survey. In the Thomas Coram Research Unit we have ourselves carried out an intensive house-to-house survey of 350 mothers of young children living in three contrasting areas of London. Despite marked differences in our three survey areas in the proportion of single-parent families, and in the proportion of middle-class parents, the data were sufficiently alike to be pooled. Social class differences in demand are remarkably small.

Table 3 presents our findings (and the OPCS data in the bottom row for comparison). It shows the number of hours parents said they would like their children to attend a pre-school centre. The proportions wanting some kind of service are almost identical with those obtained nationally.

There are several other striking features of this table. First, only a very small proportion of mothers (less than 10 per cent) would choose a centre open less than three hours a day—the duration of a session at a playgroup or a half-time

Table 3
Per cent of mothers desiring nursery services, by age of
children (Thomas Coram Research Unit Survey, 1974–5)

		Age of child				*All ages 0–4*
Hours wanted per day	*0–1*	*1–2*	*2–3*	*3–4*	*4–5*	
None	83	56	27	10	9	36
< 3	0	1	8	7	4	5
3–6	1	17	31	60	63	35
7+	16	26	(34)	23	24	24
Total desiring services (%)	17	44	73	90	91	65
OPCS National Sample	20	41	72	87	91	64

nursery school. Secondly, about one-quarter of children
would be sent to all-day care if the parents could do so,
from their second year of life. (The figure of 34 per cent for
two-year-olds is out of line here, and may be unrepresenta-
tive.) Thirdly, about 30 per cent of mothers of two-year-
olds, and more than twice as many mothers of the threes and
fours, want their children to attend a centre for at least
three hours a day—and usually for a full *school* day.

Another finding of great interest has come out of the
OPCS survey: and the data are again in accord with our own.
Only 30 per cent of parents using child minders did so from
choice—and practially no other parents would voluntarily
send their children to a minder given a choice. And of parents
of children who were at minders, only two out of three were
fully satisfied with the care the children were receiving, in
contrast to nearly all mothers with children in other forms of
day care. Clearly child minders have a poor reputation; they
aren't much liked by the parents who have to use them; and
other parents wouldn't choose to do so if they could help it.

We see, then, on the part of parents a widespread, unsatis-
fied desire for pre-school services. About one-quarter of
parents want full day care for children over one, an addi-

tional 30 per cent want full *school* day care for children from
the age of two, and 60 per cent want this for children aged
three and four. There is little enthusiasm for half-day care
for children of any age, and even less enthusiasm for child
minders.

CONTROVERSIES OVER SERVICES

I have presented at length data showing the widespread
desire on the part of parents of nursery services for young
children, because they seem to me to offer a most cogent
reaon why we should provide these services. The desire for
them has been prominent, if largely lacking expression,
throughout the whole of the last century—and there is
impressive evidence from other countries, in Western and
Eastern Europe, the American continent, Japan, Australia
and New Zealand, that a similar desire exists throughout the
industrial world. Wherever pre-school services have been provided they have been eagerly taken up, and waiting lists have
not decreased in consequence. So, many countries have now
concluded that only a service which is virtually universal in
its coverage will be adequate to meet demand. France,
Belgium and Sweden are already moving towards such a
service—at least for children over two—but none has as yet
fully achieved this target.

In Britain, however, the debate about nursery services is
still conducted in other terms: on the negative side, can we
afford pre-school services? Does separation from the mother
cause long-term harm to the child or destroy or damage the
mother and child bond? And on the positive side, the justifi-
cations offered for services are not based primarily on the
wishes of parents or consideration of the well-being of young
children, but rather on claims that nursery services reduce
social class differences by providing disadvantaged children
with a head start, and that they not only give relief to
mothers but offer opportunities for parent education. I shall
consider these arguments, but only briefly.

ECONOMIC ASPECTS

The economic issue is perhaps the one that looms largest
at the present time. Nursery services are expensive, and

labour-intensive. However there has been no real cost-analysis of them. Even during the late fifties and sixties, when there was an acute shortage of labour, no cost-benefit studies were undertaken—virtually all there is are the primitive manpower studies made during the Second World War which showed a modest gain from the provision of day nurseries in numbers of women made available for productive labour.

The situation today is very different from what it was during the Second World War and would in any case require a fresh analysis. It is worth reminding ourselves of its salient features. More women with young children are working in paid employment today than were thought able to be pressed into service in the national interest even at the height of the war; however, the wartime nurseries had exceptionally high proportions of very young children who need a high staff ratio; the numbers of single-parent families has increased in recent years and is today a prominent cause of concern; the standard of living doubled over the quarter of a century following the war, making an increase in welfare services easier to achieve; there is in contemporary Britain much more internal migration and less family and neighbourhood support for families with young children; most streets today are not safe to play in, and the flats which have replaced so many terraced houses are not good places for young children to spend the whole of their time in; the number of young children is declining as the birth-rate continues to fall; the expressed demands for a less inequitable treatment of women have received more political recognition; there are more immigrants, coming from a different culture and sometimes speaking a different language; more sophisticated methods of cost-benefit analysis have been developed; and finally both the expectation of employment by young mothers, and their consequent appraisal of themselves as unemployed if jobs are not available, raise issues of 'opportunity costs' that would require to be included in a cost-benefit analysis.

My point is not that a cost-benefit analysis would necessarily show that the marginal utility of providing comprehensive pre-school services would be greater than that of say, propping up an ailing car-manufacturing firm or supporting higher education at the level we do today: it is, rather, that

no serious analysis of costs (in the sense of opportunities for-
gone) and benefits, of different amounts and type of provision, has ever been undertaken in this field. Even when we
had full employment and were encouraging immigrants to
come into the country to work because of shortages of manpower, and even when DHSS and DES were advertising in
the papers urging women with young children to return to
nursing and teaching, no serious economic analysis of nursery
services for young children was attempted. Until this is done
it is premature to make judgements about costs and benefits.

SEPARATION FROM THE MOTHER, OR WHO KNOWS BEST?

Whether society attempts to meet the expressed wishes of
parents for nursery services for their children depends of
course partly on what it costs to do so, and the relative
importance assigned to different ways of using national resources, and partly on whether the ends are considered
socially desirable in themselves, disregarding costs. Those
who oppose nursery services argue that the best place for a
young child to grow up in is his own home with his mother.
According to this view all separation from the mother is
likely to impair or distort the child's emotional, social and
intellectual development and be destructive of the mother-
child bond. Therefore society should try to strengthen the
natural desire of parents and especially mothers to nurture
their children at home, providing material and social support
to enable them to do so. Adequate family allowances, safe
and decent housing, opportunities and facilities for young
children and mothers to meet socially in play groups and
mothers' clubs, prompt and effective treatment and support
by medical, social and psychiatric services—these are the
foundations of a good child-care policy. Nursery services, it
is claimed, not only divert resources that could be better
placed elsewhere, but are actually harmful to the child and
his mother. What is more, providing them encourages parents
to believe that it is *better* for a child to go to a nursery from
an early age. So, actively promoting the expansion of nursery
services causes mothers to deny their own instincts and part
with children whom they would otherwise cherish at home.
In other words, the critics of nursery services think that the

service does not enrich even its users but impoverishes them along with the rest of society.

No one would dispute the desirability of increasing the amount of financial, material, and social support made available to families with young children. A nursery service is only one part of what should be a comprehensive network of services designed to improve the well-being of families. Furthermore, there is every reason to believe that providing additional nursery services may well stimulate additional demand for places in them. Those who think that the proper place for a young child is at home will view this prospect with alarm. However, a closer analysis of the evidence suggests that the provision of nursery services is likely to have beneficial rather than adverse effects both on those who use them and on society. It is sometimes not appreciated that most of the evidence showing deleterious effects from separation from the mother has come from studies carried out in *residential* institutions of exceedingly poor quality. The developmental issues raised by day care are very different—and both research studies and common observation indicate that most young children settle happily in good nurseries. It is the quality of care provided which is of importance for a child's development.

There are four further considerations:

First, expert opinion abroad, and to an increasing extent in this country, supports this benign view of the value of nursery services. However, experts do disagree. But parents are overwhelmingly in favour of nursery services, and British data support the evidence from France, Belgium and Sweden, that about one-fifth of parents would make use of some form of nursery provision within the child's first year of life, two-fifths within the child's second year, three-fifths before the age of three, and over 90 per cent from three onwards. Whether in these circumstances the case against providing services can be pressed on social rather than economic grounds is highly dubious, to say the least. I think it cannot.

Secondly, the assumption that if there were adequate family allowances mothers of young children would not want to go out to work is not well supported by evidence. In France, which has an elaborate and generous system of family allowances, more young mothers are working than in Britain—and there are very many more young children in full day care. (Twenty-seven per cent of mothers of French children *under three* are in paid employment: 23 per cent of two-year-olds, 70 per cent of threes, and 93 per cent of four-year-olds are getting some form of day care.) Our surveys in Thomas Coram indicate that about four-fifths of working mothers would continue to work even if there were more money coming in to the household, though many of those working long hours (especially in unskilled occupations) would reduce their hours of work if they could afford to. However, many other mothers would work if they could be satisfied that their children could be properly cared for in their absence, so demand would probably not decrease. It seems that the desire of mothers to work is part of a profound secular change in the attitudes and expectations of women. It will not be reversed by exhortation, or even by a substantial increase in family allowances, desirable as this is on other grounds. More flexible hours, more part-time jobs, more opportunity given to mothers to take time off when children are sick—*and* increased family allowances or single-parent income supplements—would do something to change the employment patterns of parents of young children. But I do not think such measures will *substantially* change them.

The third point concerns the needy or disadvantaged, for whom there is general agreement that services should be provided. The term disadvantaged is, however, used with a variety of meanings, no one of which can claim more validity than others. Hence services which are planned to serve the needs of a section of the population defined as disadvantaged by one set of criteria, cannot provide for others who, using different criteria, would indubitably be regarded as disadvantaged—and different definitions of the term give rise to very different estimates of the proportion of families whose children are disadvantaged enough to warrant priority in nursery placement. DHSS, for example, recommends as a target for 1983 that local authorities provide 8 day nursery places per 1000 children aged 0–4. But in Britain 56 per 1000 mothers of such young children worked over 30 hours a week in 1971 and a further 81 worked more than 18 hours, or unstated hours, or were seeking employment (Moss, 1976). Many of their children must have needed, but had not been receiving, good nursery care. Or what of the young children of mothers who are psychiatrically depressed or anxious—these may be as many as one-quarter of all mothers of young children. Or children of single-parent families—260,000 aged 0–4 in Britain in 1971, 20,000 being motherless? Or children in large families? In grossly overcrowded households? In low-income families? In households where the language in the home is not English? Or handicapped children? Or children who have nowhere to play?

These groups overlap to some extent. But they are not the same groups, and the larger do not necessarily include all, or even a majority, of the children who fall into other disadvantaged categories: a service designed primarily for priority groups is bound to exclude many borderline children as well as others at least as disadvantaged by any other criteria.

A fourth problem arises when services are provided to take only very difficult or unhappy children, or those from non-supportive homes. In these circumstances staff have a hard time of it, and the children themselves are denied the opportunities to learn from other children; standards are likely to slip because the service does not come under such close and informed parental scrutiny.

These arguments put the case against selective services on the grounds that they are bound to be inadequate. Instead we should be moving towards services which are freely available. Whether or not children attend these, and (within reason) for how long each day, should be determined by the parents and not the experts: though the experts can of course advise and help parents in their decisions. Just as we want good heating in houses so that people can be warm at home in winter, and not primarily to reduce the incidence of bronchitis, and just as we want playgrounds so that children can play happily and safely, and not simply to reduce the slaughter on the roads, so we need nurseries so that children can mix with other children, enjoy themselves, be in a safe environment, and give their mothers a break.

In other words the case for nursery provision is first and

foremost a short-term one—any beneficial long-term effects may be regarded as a bonus.

THE WELL-BEING OF MOTHERS

So far I have spoken mostly about mothers; and before talking about children who, after all, are the ones for whom nursery services are provided, it is worth asking why it is that all over the industrial world mothers desire day-care services for their children. This desire is, as I have mentioned, a long-standing and apparently deep-seated one. If it is only today receiving some recognition, this is simply because the status of women has changed and more jobs have been available.

There are, however, very few countries in which more than a *minority* of mothers of young children are in paid employment, even part-time; and to discuss nursery provision solely or mainly in terms of working mothers is to concentrate on what is only part of a much more general issue concerning the status and well-being of mothers.

A number of epidemiological studies indicate very clearly that, as compared with other women, and with mothers of older children, the majority of mothers of young children can in a real sense be regarded as disadvantaged. They are more likely to be poorer and worse housed, and to have fewer services available to them than families with older children. Very many young mothers suffer from severe psychological strain, for which they tend not to seek help—probably rightly. Even so, about one in five is taking psychotropic drugs—for 'nerves'. (Not, most of them tell you, that they do them any good.) (Moss and Plewis, 1977.) A very substantial number of mothers in all social classes are worried about their children, and most mothers find the constant presence of children at times unbearable. A few are driven to such a pitch of desperation that they do their children serious injury—each year perhaps as many as 6 children in every thousand under the age of three are admitted to hospital for serious, non-accidental injury, and possibly four times as many are injured but are not reported as such (Court Report, 1976).

These are extreme instances of a much more pervasive

social sickness. The point is that though of course mothers love their children, being with them night and day is very stressful and very cramping. George Brown, a sociologist at Bedford College, London, who has made the most sensitive and extensive studies of families at different stages of the life cycle has amassed a good deal of evidence pointing to the years in which women have young children as being especially stressful. Booth, nearly a century ago, noted that it was one of the periods in which families were more likely to be in primary poverty; Brown (1975) notes the *relative* poverty of young families today—and to this adds that a very substantial number are depressed and unhappy, not necessarily because of their poverty.

A proper family policy if it existed would, no doubt, provide better housing and greatly increased family allowances and so do something to offset the *material* disadvantages of families with young children. But this would not relieve the sense of isolation and loneliness that many mothers report, nor would it necessarily decrease the great *burden* which bringing up children imposes, if this is carried by one person.

Our studies at Thomas Coram have clearly shown, as one would expect, that attendance at a nursery centre is greatly valued by *parents*. To provide universal schooling from age five but nothing as of right for younger children devalues young children, and by implication those who care for them.

ADVANTAGES TO THE CHILDREN?

Those who have been the strongest advocates of nursery services have argued that pre-school education should be supported because of its long-term benefits. Children, it is said— or used to be said—get a head start; inequalities are ironed out; healthy early growth and development are essential if optimal later development is to occur.

The issues raised by these claims are clearly too large to be adequately discussed here, but the major conclusions from a wealth of research in child development and early child education can I think be summarized briefly (Tizard, 1976).

First, attendance at traditional nursery school makes very little difference to a child's later IQ or educational progress in primary school. Secondly, structured programmes introduced into nursery schools *can* give a modest lift to a child's competence, though the effects, like those of a permanent wave, wash out or grow out in time. Thirdly, it is by no means certain that disadvantaged children, however defined, benefit more than children from more privileged homes. What we know of other aspects of development might support the view that environmental enrichment is likely to increase rather than diminish differences in competencies which are in part an expression of innate potential. But even if this were so, what bearing does it have on the issue? Primary schools have not been shown to be great levellers, but no one says that they should therefore be closed down. And no one to my knowledge has ever applied this argument to universities. (On the other hand it is obvious that an educationally appropriate milieu can reduce or even eliminate *some* kinds of disadvantage: if a child from a non-English-speaking home learns English in nursery school he is obviously better off, if he lives in England, both at the time and when he starts primary school.)

Fourthly, it has been shown that many educational programmes introduced in nursery settings, though ostensibly different both in aim and in content, have had largely comparable effects. (Possibly they differ less in practice than their designers would have us believe.) Fifthly, some programmes, and some nursery milieux, *have* been shown to have a remarkably powerful effect upon children's competencies.

This facilitating effect of specific programmes can come about in several ways: children can, for example, be taught very difficult skills like how to play the violin, or gymnastics, or swimming, or long passages of the Koran, or how to draw and paint, or a second language. We also know that in a more general way differences in the nursery environment do profoundly influence children's development. Thus children in *good* residential nurseries talk and understand speech like ordinary children of ordinary working-class parents; but children in *very* good ones, linguistically speaking, talk and understand speech like children of professional parents. Again, children who are brought up at home by mothers with

IQs less than 70 have IQs of about 95 between the ages of two and six; but similar children who attend a stimulating all-day nursery centre from early infancy have IQs of 120. These and other data show that environmental differences, if great enough, *can* result in profound differences in competencies. And most experimental programmes have shown only modest effects because they have, after all, been modest forms of intervention.

We don't know a great deal about the effects of nursery attendance on social and emotional development—this has not been studied very systematically. What data there are support both the cognitive findings and common observation: children tend to adjust to the standards of the group they are in, and model their behaviour on their peers and the adults who look after them. So where expectations of behaviour are very different from ours (as in Chinese nurseries for example) norms of behaviour are very different also.

This is not a very dramatic set of findings, perhaps. My point is, however, that none of them give—or should give—decisive support either to the advocates or to the opponents of nursery services, though they *ought* to influence our planning of the nursery day.

We come back therefore to what I regard as the central considerations affecting decisions wether or not to expand the nursery programme: a large proportion of mothers are weighed down by the constant care of young children and are frustrated and unhappy; nearly all children enjoy nursery experience; most parents desire this for their children, at least from the age of two. These are widespread and enduring patterns of behaviour, not just current problems and fads. To satisfy these very reasonable demands should be a major objective of social policy.

Research in child development has contributed rather little to the practice of early education and child care, because, I believe, the central problems of nursery services seem to be not those which have been most studied. They arise rather, in the context of other problems: how can we best organize a nursery service? How can we best staff it? What should we teach young children and how? Only the last of these is primarily a problem which draws much upon developmental psychology, though any services we provide do of course have to take the developmental characteristics of children into account. However in western society we must recognize that it is from differences in the organizational structure and staffing of our nursery services that the major differences in patterns of care and education arise; only when we get the structure of our service right will we be able to tackle the fascinating problems of curriculum. So I shall say only this about curriculum: that Bruner's (1960) most widely quoted dictum—that any subject can be taught effectively in some intellectually honest form to any child at any stage of development—could well form the starting-point for any discussion of what we should plan for in the nursery school.

HOW CAN WE ORGANIZE SERVICES?

The first *policy* decision then is as to how we can best organize a nursery service. The problem is being discussed throughout the industrial world, and we can get ideas from what is happening abroad as well as from what is going on here. Let's look at the issues, and the choices.

The main requirements of a nursery service can be stated simply. Here are six, and they apply both to 'selective' and to 'universal' services (Tizard, Moss and Perry, 1976).

First, the service should meet the needs of the children. It should be emotionally and socially supportive, with continuity of staffing, and intellectually geared to the child's developing needs and competencies. Young children are best cared for in small groups. The physical environment should be safe, warm, and attractive both to children and staff.

Secondly, the service should be locally based—preferably near the children's homes, less desirably near the place of work of a parent who will deliver and collect. A locally based service is one within easy pram-pushing distance with a toddler in tow. Not very far, and not across busy roads.

Thirdly, the service should ensure that the child's educational and welfare needs are provided for. It is unsatisfactory to divide education from care, to oblige children in day nurseries, for example, to traipse off to a nearby nursery school for their education, or to regard only nursery schools as having an educational function. In our divided service the difference between education and child care is made much of because it does not upset existing professional structures: but a sharp distinction between teaching and caring is not something one would plan, if one started with the well-being of the *children*.

Fourthly, an integrated nursery centre will also have its doctor and nurse calling regularly, and function both as an infant welfare centre and as a surgery where children can be given primary medical care; the clinic should not be simply a diagnostic centre from which children are referred to a G.P. or hospital for treatment which does not demand special facilities.

Fifthly, a nursery service should, I think, be seen as being as much a part of the educational service as are schools. This means it should be free. At the very least there should not be economic bariers to attendance. A compromise might be the French system of *écoles maternelles*, open from 8 till 6.30. Here the educational component last six hours and is free. Those whose children come before school starts, or stay on afterwards, pay a fee.

Finally the parents should participate in the management and the day-to-day running of the service. Sometimes we forget today that doctors and nurses, teachers, social workers and nursery nurses, psychologists and therapists, and administrators, are the servants of their clients, not their masters.

Accepting objectives such as these, what are the choices open to us?

THE PRESENT SYSTEM

The present system is an outcome of history and is neither rational nor functional. Both centrally and locally provision is the responsibility of two departments—social services and education. Coordination between them is more talked about than practised, and the supply of services is a poor fit with need, however defined. Parents don't in fact have much choice at all in what they are offered, and about one mother in five, according to the OPCS national survey, doesn't feel she knows enough about how the child is getting on at the nursery, school, child minder—or playgroup.

The same survey has given data about the mismatch

between parental desire to participate more in the running of their children's nurseries and the extent to which they actually do. About half of all parents, including those whose children are at playgroups, would prefer to leave things to those who run them; and nearly two-thirds (and about half of those with children at playgroups) never in fact spend any time there. This was often because they felt they weren't welcome—only half of all mothers, and only two-thirds of those with children at playgroups, felt they were welcome there—a revealing comment.

What we see then is that some mothers are being drawn reluctantly into the running of playgroups which they would prefer to leave to others to run; in all the other services, and among mothers whose children don't at present attend, there is a very substantial unfulfilled desire on the part of parents to participate. Overall, a minority of mothers, and maybe fathers, are keen to be drawn into work with young children. But even in playgroups they don't necessarily have much choice as to whether they are.

Is it feasible, however, to think that, if sufficient financial support and help with premises were made available, a largely voluntary movement such as the playgroup movement could make good much of the shortfall in our present services, and hopefully at less cost than a professional service? I doubt it.

PLAYGROUPS

The spectacular growth of the playgroup movement should not blind us to its inadequacies. Apart from problems over money and premises, which could be put right, there are two. The first relates to the time playgroups are open—half-day sessions. These are of course of no use to working mothers, even those who work part-time. In 1971 one mother in five of a young child was employed and numbers may well have risen since—in the national OPCS survey in 1974 the proportion was 26 per cent and in our survey of 1975 it was 44 per cent in London. And part-time services are not very popular with other mothers either, as we have seen.

The other structural problem of playgroups is that of achieving continuity. A voluntary group, especially a parent one centred mainly on three- and four-year-old children, is essentially unstable. As the children move into primary school parental interest shifts from the playgroup to the school, the activists drop out and new activists have to be recruited. Often this is not possible; and without professional support, continuity of organization and staffing is difficult or impossible to maintain.

The playgroup movement has tackled this by an excellent training programme for play leaders. This is undoubtedly working well—at present. But there are tensions between professionals and volunteers; and playgroup leaders have an indeterminate status, as very badly paid quasi-professionals with no career prospects. The situation is organizationally fragile: cracks already apparent will I believe within the next few years be seen as being caused by serious structural faults. The only satisfactory solution is, I think, to be found in institutions which have a mixed staffing structure of professionals and volunteers working together. This, and the provision of all-day services are the two major issues facing the playgroup movement as I see it.

CHILD MINDERS

A second low-cost proposal for child care is through a vast increase in the child-minding service, backed up by local authority support.

From the OPCS survey figures it appears likely that today in England and Wales over 100,000 children under 5 are being child minded at any one time—2 per cent of infants under 1 (or about 15,000) and 3 per cent of children aged 1-4 (over 90,000). In our local surveys of Bloomsbury and Paddington we, in Thomas Coram Research Unit, have found much the same proportions, though five times as many children (14 per cent) have been minded at some point in the past. This brings out the first serious problem of child minding—the instability of the relationship. By and large child minding is practised primarily in the interest of the minder, rather than the child. On the whole it is badly paid; and the relationship between minder and parent is an uneasy one, soured by commercialism and fear of bad debts. It is not an arrangement liked by parents, and there is no doubt that many children are very badly looked after by minders.

Mayall and Petrie (1977) of the Thomas Coram Research Unit, who are at present studying registered child minders recommended by the local authority because they have satisfactorily minded a child for at least a year, have noted other shortcomings. In general, it appears, the minder does not provide the intimate relationship with her charges that some people have claimed to be the outstanding advantage of this domestic form of care. Children tend to be ignored, told to get on with their play, not talked to much. They are quieter and more subdued than children in nurseries. The play facilities tend to be inadequate, the accommodation used for other purposes, the minders as harassed as the mothers whose children they are minding. The present training schemes being tried out by some local authorities appear, on the basis of such slight evidence as we have, to be wholly ineffectual.

Mrs. Petrie has made proposals to improve the situation. They include compulsory training; employment by the local council; adequate pay; insurance against accidents; allocation of ground-floor housing with access to out-of-door play space; at least one room set aside for the children's exclusive use; an adequate toy and meals allowance; and domestic assistance. Most minders should work in twos, to increase numbers and provide continuity and relief over holidays and sickness. There should be an association with a local primary school, with a local playgroup, and with the child welfare clinic. Proper supervision should be provided by the local authority, which should have educators appointed for this purpose.

A system like this would resemble the family crèche system in France and Belgium, or the family day nursery system of Sweden. It is, however, noteworthy that in these countries this form of provision is giving way to organized nursery centre care, except for the small numbers of children under two for whom full-day care is needed.

In short, child minding, though it sounds all right, commends itself to government mainly because it promises services on the cheap. It flourishes because of the exploitation of women (we never think of trying to attract men to such a badly paid and unattractive service); and the very term to describe it—child minding—is indicative of the attitude we take to it, and to the children who come to be so 'minded'. Of course it has the advantage of cheapness, flexibility of hours, and potentially of proximity to parents. But a properly organized child-minding service—one we would send our own children to as we would to a nursery school—would not be cheap, and would not necessarily offer advantages over other, better organized, forms of care.

Child minding should I think have a very minor part to play in a comprehensive service, and be part of the services administered and financed by the local authority.

LOCAL AUTHORITY DAY NURSERIES, PRIVATE NURSERIES, AND NURSERY SCHOOLS

Day nurseries and nursery schools and classes are the major forms of provision in Britain which provide exclusively for children under the age of five and which are professionally staffed.

Each of these services fulfils more or less adequately, for those children who attend, the objects it sets itself. But of course it makes no sense to have two separate services; and each one serves only a small fraction of the need.

In Britain joint action to provide a combined day-care and education service takes two forms. Some day nurseries send selected children to nursery schools for half-day sessions; and there is a small number of centres which combine a day nursery and a nursery school. These are intended to function so as to ensure the harmonious development of mind and body.

In practice neither of these arrangements is satisfactory. Psychologically it seems odd that professionals who talk so much about the young child's need for continuity of care should favour sending young, deprived children to nursery school for a part of the day in order to get educational play which might be better provided in the day nursery. The consequence for the child is that he moves from home, to nursery, to nursery school, to nursery, to home all in the course of a day, and is required to adjust to two sets of adults and children outside the family, and not just one. But the alternative of having a nursery school, nursery class, or just a nursery teacher in the day nursery is disturbing to staff;

it confronts them every day with the fact that teachers work a 25-hour week for 40 weeks a year for much more pay than nursery nurses; they work 38 hours a week for 48 weeks a year doing, as it must seem to them, much the same job but for much less pay and over much longer hours. This is a structural problem. And until it is solved, which can only be by an integrated day-care and education service as has been proposed in France and Sweden, 'combined' services are bound to be in a state of friction, or to decide through unspoken agreement to run as two entirely separate services which share premises. All this has long been as plain as a pikestaff, but it isn't spoken about much, and no local authority *does* anything about it because to do so would cut across administrative boundaries.

Though inter-department committees of various sorts are said to function in a feeble way, centrally and in some instances locally, the problems are not soluble within existing departmental structures—save in exceptional circumstances when a determined head (more rarely two determined and like-thinking heads) imposes a structure on the centres which cuts across the boundaries of education and care. What is required therefore is a new Inter-Departmental Committee to review the whole of the organization, staffing, and objectives of our services for children under the age of five, or, better, the age of eight.

AN INTEGRATED NURSERY SERVICE

An integrated day-care and education centre, under a single head and serving a defined catchment area within pram-pushing distance, does offer an attractive solution to the organizational problems of caring for and educating young children who live near by. The centre could and should also serve as a child health clinic, able to treat medically as well as diagnose and prescribe. In France and in Sweden such centres are being established, and in my research unit we are working with colleagues in the Thomas Coram Children's Centre in Bloomsbury and the Dorothy Gardner Centre in Paddington who are developing two centres of this kind.

One could imagine further extensions of this type of

organization: a larger children's centre with smaller, more domestic centres serving perhaps single streets or single blocks of flats; or a centre linked with paid child minders in the neighbourhood who worked perhaps in pairs and who had ready access to the centre, as Mrs. Petrie has proposed. The larger centres could, and should, have units for handicapped children, adequately staffed and with ready access to paediatric, psychological and other specialist services.

One might hope too that if the divisional boundaries between professions could be obliterated, and if professionals could be persuaded to work more with parents, the miracle performed by the playgroup movement in unleashing the enormous energy and enthusiasm of parents might be repeated—to the benefit of teachers, parents, and—above all—children.

NURSERY AND RECEPTION CLASSES IN PRIMARY SCHOOLS

An expansion of nursery centres of the type I have sketched seems to me the best form that development could take. But this isn't likely to happen, at least during the next few years, and it may be useful therefore to consider the alternatives. Perhaps the most feasible is a development of the system of nursery classes in primary schools, already by far the most significant sector of public provision. In some schools arrangements are already made for the care of children after school hours. These arrangements are, however, for the most part somewhat hit and miss. A more formal system along the lines of the French *école maternelle* would be by no means impossible to introduce, and would be comparatively cheap. And the decline in the number of children of school age—in Britain perhaps 1·3 million fewer in 1981 than in 1974—could free classrooms and teachers to work as *éducateurs* rather than *instructeurs*, as play leaders and community organizers on behalf of children rather than as pedagogues.

Nursery units in primary schools offer another advantage in that they don't make it necessary for the child to have a break in his schooling at the age of five. The decision to make five the age for compulsory schooling was taken over a century ago, at a time when there was in any case no barrier to children starting earlier, and when there was no other form of publicly supported educational service for young children. Today most psychologists and educators believe that five is not a good age at which to transfer to another school—seven is thought to be better. And even though it would be hard to convince a sceptic that this is so, it would make things easier for parents of more than one young child to have them at the same centre, and would help younger sibs to settle in there.

Organizationally speaking, however, there is no *one* right way of developing our services for young children—though there are many poor models, most of them well represented in British practice. We would be wise to try out a lot of new things; and a function which research and demonstration projects could usefully fulfil would be to undertake both comparative and experimental studies to explore the shortcomings and potentialities of different models, and study ways in which they could be made to function better. The main task, however, is to *extend* the services, recognizing that this cannot be done on the cheap.

SUMMARY AND CONCLUSIONS

(1) I do not share the widely held view that we have no choice but to cut back on the nursery programme and concentrate on 'selective' services. Nor do I think that an expansion of child minding and playgroups will take us far towards the solution of the pressing problems of the under fives and their families. The cuts are being justified on economic grounds; but they also reflect political priorities (cf. Concorde). At the least, an expansion of the nursery programme would both create many jobs and release even larger numbers of women for productive employment—as was shown during the Second World War. Without a cost-benefit analysis even the economic case for cuts remains unproven.

(2) We know that very many mothers of young children have an exceedingly hard time of it, and that nursery services are a boon both to them and to their children. The OPCS study indicates the extent of unmet desire for services; our own more intensive studies at the Thomas Coram Research Unit fully corroborate these findings and indicate that a

nursery service that provides in an integrated way for the health, education, and welfare (day care) needs of young children is of great value to mothers as well as children. Several surveys have shown that among the working-class mothers of young children two in every five suffer from depression, anxiety, and low self-esteem. The constant strain of child care is in part, and perhaps in large part, responsible. The seriousness of the position of families with young children, especially mothers, has been largely ignored.

(3) It has been said that if we provided adequate child allowances, as they do in France, there would be no need for mothers to work: they could stay at home and enjoy their children. The facts are that though France has the best system of family benefits in Western Europe and perhaps the world it *also* has a very high rate of employment among mothers of young children (27 per cent of mothers of children under *three* are employed.) Furthermore, in France very large numbers of children attend pre-school facilities (25 per cent of two-year-olds, 70 per cent of three and practically all fours and fives). Nurseries are often open from 8 a.m. to 6.30 p.m. and full-day care is much commoner than it is here.

This suggests that women go out to work for reasons other than purely financial ones; giving family benefits does not guarantee that women will choose to stay at home with their young children—indeed both in continental Europe and in Britain mothers in the upper, more prosperous classes are more likely to be working than wives of skilled manual workers while their children are still very young.

(4) The view that separation from the mother is harmful is based largely upon studies carried out in *residential* institutions of poor quality. Day care poses different questions. The effects of all forms of care, whether at home or in nurseries, depend upon the quality and consistency of the caring. At all events experts are divided in their views about whether day care has bad effects—at the time, or for later life—and to cite 'expert opinion' as grounds for discouraging a nursery programme is unjustified. The much more highly developed health, education and welfare programmes for young children in some other Western European coun-

tries—to go no further—reflect a public concern which shows itself in more tangible form than does our own. It is also at least as well informed.

(5) The playgroup movement has been an example to all professionals in demonstrating the enormous reserve of talent and energy available at the community level, which can be used to benefit young children—and many parents. As the OPCS survey shows, however, most mothers desire longer hours, and many participate rather reluctantly. In their present form, then, playgroups cannot meet the expressed demand for day care. Moreover playgroup leaders are extremely badly paid and, despite small local authority grants, much of their money comes from extensive fund-raising activities. I believe that playgroups should be given increasing support from public funds. This, however, should not just be handed out indiscriminately, but with a view to extending the hours available (e.g. by providing lunches at least), increasing the wages of playleaders, and improving premises and equipment. Moreover very much more support and encouragement should be given to other forms of community-based provision, such as all-day nurseries run by voluntary bodies but staffed by properly paid workers. Generous support of this nature is much more readily available on the Continent than in Britain.

(6) Very few mothers would make a *child-minder* their first choice; those who do use them are far less satisfied than mothers using other services. Our own studies of registered minders are in keeping with this evidence: even where the physical environment is fairly satisfactory, the minders rarely offer a close mothering relationship to the child—though this has frequently been put forward as their main strength.

Most child-minders do the job for their own convenience—often short-term—because it fits with their domestic commitments, not out of informed, caring interest in children. The very poor rates of pay are an indication of their low and exploited status, and of the residual nature of the job. So training schemes carried out by local authorities are unlikely to affect the attitudes of those currently minding, who have nothing to gain by improving the way they 'mind' children.

The turnover of children who are 'minded' is disturbingly high and is likely to remain so unless child minding becomes a profession or quasi-profession. I think it should, but foresee only a minor part for it in a properly organized pre-school service. It should be under the close supervision and control of the Local Authority. This would of course make it a much more expensive service.

(7) Since the majority of mothers of young children are not economically active it is a mistake to equate pre-school services with working mothers. None the less the Department of Employment and employers should have an obligation to ensure that adequate child-care arrangements are made for the young children of all employed mothers. DHSS ought to give a lead here by inquiring into the situation affecting hospital staff.

(8) One group of children for whom services should be provided as a matter of priority are young handicapped children. The numbers are not large. The very great majority are, I believe, best placed in ordinary nursery schools and day nurseries. However, if this is done, the nurseries should be properly equipped and staffed to cater for their special needs, and there should be regular and frequent contacts with consultant paediatric, psychological social and educational services at district level.

(9) More generally, expansion could, I believe, best take place through the development of integrated nursery centres offering medical services, and education and full- and part-time day care as desired by parents—with parent participation and involvement. Such centres should serve small local communities, To them could be attached smaller 'satellite' centres of a domestic type, and perhaps day foster homes for which they could provide advice and back-up services.

A more feasible alternative in hard times, and one that offers some advantages in any case, is through a major expansion of nursery classes (cf. French *écoles maternelles*).

(10) Finally, though one can distinguish the care from the education of young children it by no means follows that only caretakers can give care, and only educators can give education. The division of nursery services between two Departments does not make sense. We need an independent, Inter-

Departmental Committee to look at the objectives, structure, staffing, and content of our nursery services, with a view to making recommendations as to how a unified service for young children, supervised by one authority, can best be achieved.

REFERENCES

BONE, M., 'Day care for pre-school children.' In *Low Cost Day Provision for the Under-Fives*. (Papers from a Conference held at the Civil Service College, Sunningdale Park, 9—10 January, 1976.) Uxbridge, Middlesex: Brunel University, 1976.

BROWN, G., BHROLCHAIN, M. and HARRIS, T., 'Social class and psychiatric disturbance among women in an urban population.' *Sociology*, 9, 225—54. 1975.

BRUNER, J. S., *The Process of Education*. Cambridge: Harvard University Press, 1960.

CENTRAL ADVISORY COUNCIL FOR EDUCATION (ENGLAND), *Children and Their Primary Schools*. (Plowden Report.) London: H.M.S.O., 1967.

COMMITTEE ON CHILD HEALTH SERVICES, *Fit for the Future: The Report of the Committee on Child Health Services*. (Chairman, D. Court.) London: H.M.S.O. (Cmnd. 6684), 1976.

COMMITTEE ON ONE-PARENT FAMILIES, Report of the Committee. (Finer Report.) London: H.M.S.O., 1974.

FERGUSON, S. and FITZGERALD, H., *Studies in the Social Services*. London: H.M.S.O., 1954.

GATHORNE-HARDY, J., *The Rise and Fall of the British Nanny*. London: Hodder and Stoughton, 1972.

MAYALL, B. and PETRIE, P., *Minder, Mother and Child*. London: University of London, Institute of Education, 1977.

MOSS, P., 'The current situation.' In N. Fonda and P. Moss (eds.), *Mothers in Employment: Trends and Issues*. Uxbridge, Middlesex: Brunel University, 1976.

MOSS, P. and PLEWIS, I., 'Mental distress in mothers of pre-school children.' *Psychological Medicine*, 1977, in press.

TIZARD, J. 'The effects of day care on young children.' In N. Fonda and P. Moss (eds.), *Mothers in Employment: Trends and Issues*. Uxbridge, Middlesex: Brunel University, 1976.

TIZARD, J., MOSS, P. and PERRY, J., *All Our Children: Preschool Services in a Changing Society*. London: Maurice Temple Smith, 1976.